Educating Men and Women Together

Educating Men and Women Together:
Coeducation in a Changing World

Edited by
CAROL LASSER

**Published by the University of Illinois Press
in conjunction with Oberlin College**
Urbana and Chicago

© 1987 by the Board of Trustees of the University of Illinois
Manufactured in the United States of America
C 5 4 3 2 1

This book is printed on acid-free paper.

Library of Congress Cataloging-in-Publication Data

Educating men and women together.

Based on essays presented at a conference held at
Oberlin College in Oberlin, Ohio, Mar. 11–13, 1983.
  Includes bibliographies and index.
  1. Coeducation—United States—Congresses.
2. Oberlin College—Students—History—Congresses.
I. Lasser, Carol.
LC1601.E38   1987   376   86–7126
ISBN 0-252-01346-8 (alk. paper)

In memory of Janet Harley

Contents

Acknowledgments

Many members of the Oberlin College community deserve thanks for making possible the gathering at which these essays were first presented. I note particularly the efforts of former Acting President James Powell, Associate Dean David Love, Director of Capital Development and Chair of the Sesquicentennial Celebration Committee David Clark, and the late Phyllis Jones for their early support of the project. My fellow members of the Oberlin College Sesquicentennial Coeducation Conference Committee worked hard to bring together a stimulating program and to make the conference itself a success. I thank Frank Laycock, Katherine Linehan, Marlene Merrill, Edith Swan, and student member Kiran Chadhuri. I am particularly grateful to my committee co-chair, Geoffrey Blodgett. Sesquicentennial Staff Coordinator Mary Durling made many difficult tasks easier during the planning and celebration and in its aftermath.

Several individuals presented papers at the Oberlin Conference that do not appear in this volume; their work nonetheless made the conference and this publication a better one. I thank Alice Ilchman, Elizabeth Minnich, Robert Staples, and acknowledge the contributions of the late Joe L. Dubbert and the late John William Ward.

I also thank Charlotte Briggs and Kimberly Brookes for cheerful research and secretarial assistance, and April Paramore for aid in preparing the manuscript. Sandra Peacock undertook a wide variety of tasks on this volume and provided some fine editorial assistance. She helped me to see the work as possible; I applaud her decision to return to her own academic career.

I am especially grateful to Mr. and Mrs. Roy G. Harley (Jane Edwards, '38), who generously supported this project in memory of their daughter, Janet Harley, wife of Wesley Collins.

Finally, I thank Gary Kornblith and Russell Lasser Kornblith, who make my own household "coeducational," and, in doing so, nurture my understanding of the relations between the sexes.

Introduction

CAROL LASSER

"*Resolved* That after more than two years experience in the plan of Uniting a male and female department in the same Institute we are amply sustained in the opinion that the mutual influence of the sexes upon each other is decidedly happy in the cultivation of both mind & manners, and that its effect in promoting real virtue and in correcting the irregularities, frivolities & follies common to youth is unquestionably beneficial."[1] Thus read the first evaluation of the experiment in the "joint education of the sexes" undertaken by the Oberlin Collegiate Institute. Nearly 150 years later, the college decided to commemorate the anniversary of its 1833 founding by examining seriously the ramifications of the task it had undertaken when it permitted women equal access to all aspects of the education it provided to men, including, in 1837, the fledging institute's collegiate course.[2]

This retrospective examination of coeducation in America, joined by the scholars who have contributed to this book, came at the end of two decades of rapid movement toward coeducation by the nation's most prestigious educational institutions. The proportion of single-sex colleges and universities dropped from nearly 25 percent to a mere 6 percent, with only some 3 percent excluding women.[3] Most notably, all of the prestigious Ivy League colleges determined to admit women, beginning with Yale's decision in 1969 and concluding with the enrollment of female students in Columbia College in the fall of 1983. Thus the value of coeducation, its success and failures in supplying equal education, its

1

utility and significance, all are matters of the greatest interest for contemporary educators.

Until quite recently, advocates and critics alike unquestioningly held equal education for women and men to be synonymous with coeducation. In the nineteenth century, woman's rights leaders, including Elizabeth Cady Stanton and Susan B. Anthony—and Oberlin graduates Lucy Stone and Antoinette Brown Blackwell—assumed that women would attain premium quality education only when they gained access to the well-endowed and prestigious educational facilities then enjoyed exclusively by men. As woman's rights advocate Caroline Dall explained, "We claim for women a share of the [academic] opportunities offered to men, because we believe that they will never be thoroughly taught until they are taught at the same time and in the same classes."[4] Their opponents feared that giving women access to men's education would rob women of their distinctive feminine attributes, including their reproductive capacities.[5] Nonetheless, slowly, and often for reasons of economy and geography rather than ideology, women gained access to the majority of institutions of higher education.

By the mid-1960s, only a relatively small number of colleges remained single-sex, yet among them were the well-known and insistently male colleges of the Ivy League. Focusing on these prestigious institutions in particular, the emergent women's movement declared the justice of opening to women all the educational facilities in the nation. These feminists were gratified when shortly thereafter single-sex institutions at first hesitantly and then overwhelmingly moved toward coeducation. Many, like the formerly all-male Lafayette College in Easton, Pennsylvania, professed their discovery of an egalitarian mission, declaring, "There is no denying that sexually segregated colleges came into being in a male-dominated society, and there are no sound educational arguments to support their continued existence in a society that is no longer so extremely sexually segregated."[6] Even superior women's colleges felt that equal access to the classroom served both sexes better; as Connecticut College president Charles E. Shain noted, there was a "growing conviction that in this age, a young American's education, when it is shared with the opposite sex, *is superior in its basic learning conditions* to an education in a single-sex environment."[7]

Yet by the time the last of the Ivy-League gates had swung open to welcome women to Columbia, educators and scholars had new information and were formulating new assessments of the impact of coeducation.

Many of them were no longer convinced that women received the best education when they studied beside their male peers. Further, they recognized that entrance frequently did not seem to alter the attitudes of administrators or instructors toward women, nor did it assure the equal treatment of women within the institution, and the curriculum at previously all-male schools did not always appear to serve the best interests of newly admitted women. In short, as women gained equal access to more institutions, it became clear that their presence alone did not insure the innovations necessary to provide them with truly equal educations.

In evaluating the success of coeducation during this decade of change, proponents and critics from a variety of disciplinary backgrounds with a broad array of ideological commitments investigated a wide range of issues. They looked into sex ratios, dating patterns, grade distributions, admissions statistics, and even recreational and health facilities. In the end, however, their questions basically clustered in three related categories: first, the extent to which the entrance of women into coeducational institutions was motivated by feminist concerns; second, the impact of coeducation on the academic and career aspirations of women students; and third, the value to women of the content of the education to which they had gained access. Motives, impact, and content, then, formed the core of the inquiry into the success of coeducation.

The first area of inquiry, the reevaluation of the reasons for which educators and administrators had promoted the growth of coeducation, developed in part from the careful reconsideration of the 150-year history of the movement toward placing men and women side by side in the classroom. Principled arguments favoring coeducation were first articulated long before the experiment began in earnest with the admission of women to Oberlin's collegiate course. Assuming, as Mary Wollstonecraft had argued, that the mind had no "sexual character,"[8] proponents of coeducation asserted that providing women with an equal education meant providing them with the same education at the same time in the same place. But other logic, less conerened with the progress of women toward equality, had also actuated some of those who secured for women access to the education provided for men. One set of arguments stressed the benefits *for men* of having women's moral influence exerted in classrooms and on campuses. Another more crassly materialistic line of thought noted the economy achieved by providing only one set of facilities to be used jointly by both sexes.

The findings of historians who carefully studied the early chapters in the development of coeducation reinforced the suspicions of contemporary educators who discovered similar cynical motives for the more recent moves toward coeducation. Economy, better utilization of facilities and faculties, and improvements in the quality of social life often loomed large in the reports issued by institutions undertaking sexual integration in the early 1970s. By the end of this decade, scholars in a variety of fields hotly debated the extent to which both past and present advocates of coeducation had ever intended to promote the equality of women.[9]

Closely related to the question of motives was the second area of inquiry into coeducation: the impact of coeducation on women students. Clearly, if equality had never been the intention of those who allowed the entrance of women into coeducational classrooms, then it was not surprising when women found it difficult to elevate their status within those learning environments. However, investigators also began to ask whether, even when sincere egalitarian motives had brought about sexual integration, simply sitting women next to men in the same classes and on the same campuses could actually provide the sexes with truly equal education. Some critics charged that the norms of female inferiority and subordination ineluctably find their ways into the coeducational college so long as sexism pervades society. Studies of the impact of gender bias on the educational experience of women have provided data on the subtle but ubiquitous messages received in contacts with male fellow students, teachers, and administrators.[10] In addition, other research has explored why women graduates of single-sex institutions have a greater likelihood of achieving prominence in their occupations and are more likely to earn higher degrees than the alumnae of coeducational institutions.[11] The findings of these contemporary analysts fostered in some critics a pessimistic appraisal of the value of access. Why, they questioned, expend the effort to achieve access for women to situations in which their subordinate status is reinforced? Why not instead foster the growth of separate institutions?

Such thinking does not, however, address constructively the current situation. It is unlikely that any sexually integrated college or university will eliminate coeducation in order to promote women's education or to avoid the difficulties it generates. But these doubts have stimulated creative thinking, particularly in reevaluating the content of the education to which women have increasingly gained access. The investigation of the extent to which the curriculum of higher education has been a gendered curriculum, largely created by men to serve men, and reinforcing the gender assumptions and gender biases of society, has drawn to it a provocative set of thinkers. The issue, however, is hardly new. Fifty years ago Virginia Woolf noted that, traditionally, colleges taught their students "the arts of dominating other people; . . . the arts of ruling, of killing, of acquiring land and capital,"[12] skills Woolf found inappropriate for women, if not for all people, to learn. Today, a growing body of scholarship asserts that, even in the "gentler" fields of literature, art, or music, the scholar and the student are presumed to be male, and the works of culture are presumed to be created and maintained by men for predominantly male audiences. The invisibility of the past achievements of women—as individuals and as a group—create for the female student a sense of her status as outsider. The absence of both the study of women and a woman's perspective on the broad range of academic studies has impoverished the content as well as the orientation of scholarship. Such omissions are more glaring and yet also more subtle in a coeducational context where women are invited to participate in the academic life "just like" men.

Many educational theorists have suggested that content on women needs to become part of the coeducational curriculum, either through specifically focused women's studies courses or through mainstreaming this material into the general educational program. Others, in some ways more radical, have stressed that in an age where human survival itself is at stake, traditionally female values like cooperation and nurturance must become part of higher education for the sake of both men and women. The poet and thinker Adrienne Rich typifies this radical position when she asks pointedly whether higher education, "this male-created, male-dominated structure [,] is really capable of serving the humanism and freedom it professes."[13] In response to such concerns, many institutions have funded faculty, curricular programs, and research centers to complement coeducation by finding places for materials by and about women, as well as alternative values, within the structures of higher education. Their opponents often question whether such activities are actually legitimate academic endeavors, insisting that politics and pedagogy must remain separate. The debate over the proper relationship between the content of higher education and the quest for equality between the sexes therefore remains an area of heated controversy.

These three concerns—motives, outcomes, and content—thus remain key areas of inquiry in the study of coeducation and its past, present, and future. The purest of motives have not always actuated those with the power to provide women with access to men's education, nor has such access proved to be a solution to all the problems of educational equity. As women have accepted uncritically the traditional education to which they have gained entrance, it has too often been at the cost of the critical tools that women as outsiders can bring to a predominantly male culture. Yet despite the persistence of such prodigious difficulties, the enormous significance of the achievement of access by women to all aspects of higher education, as teachers and administrators, as students and staff, should not be ignored. And the overwhelming proportion of that access has been achieved in coeducational institutions, which must now take up the task of exploring the innovations necessary, in the content, structure, and values of their educational programs, to fulfill the promise of true educational equity for men and women.

This volume, which presents essays growing out of the Oberlin Sesquicentennial Conference on Coeducation, sheds further light on the past, present, and future of the challenge of coeducation. It opens with a provocative essay in which Alice Rossi questions how to measure the success of coeducation. The next section contains two essays that examine the historical evolution of arguments in favor of women's education and the resulting growth of women's access to education, at first primarily in single-sex institutions.

The history of Oberlin, the first coeducational college, serves as a focal point for the third section, which examines the motives and the success of the historic experiment in the "joint education of the sexes." The fourth section raises a set of difficult issues facing administrators and educators who would provide equal education to men and women in the same institutions today; such challenges include, but are not limited to, the adaptations of both men and women to the gender revolution as well as the sexual revolution, the significance of the interaction of race and sex, and the issue of sexual orientation. The volume concludes with Catharine Stimpson's stimulating case for the need for innovation within contemporary coeducational institutions.

By exploring the original context in which the questions of coeducation first emerged, then tracing the early history and impact of the "joint education of the sexes," by offering an analysis of several of the contemporary challenges to coeducation, and finally by pointing out the necessity for change in order to retain the progressive nature of coeducation, this volume invites administrators and educators, scholars and students, to view higher education with fresh eyes and new information. It reaches beyond the Oberlin experiment to the wide variety of institutions and individuals with an interest in coeducation today. This collection of essays should stimulate a genuine "re-vision" of the methods and objectives necessary to create a truly equal education for men and women. Perhaps it will stimulate innovative thinking about the challenges coeducation faces today.

NOTES

In addition to my appreciation for the efforts made by all the participants in the Oberlin Sesquicentennial Conference and the valuable conversations held with members of the Conference Planning Committee, I thank especially Gary Kornblith, Katherine Linehan, and Marlene Deahl Merrill for their assistance in preparing this essay.

1. MS Minutes of the Board of Trustees of the Oberlin Collegiate Institute, March 9, 1836, quoted in Robert S. Fletcher, *A History of Oberlin College from Its Foundation through the Civil War*, 2 vols. (Oberlin, Ohio: Oberlin College, 1943), I: 377.

2. The provision of access for women to the institute's theological course was not tested until 1847 when two women, Antoinette Brown (later Blackwell) and Lettice Smith Holmes, attended its classes, although neither was accorded recognition as a graduate of this program when she completed the course of study three years later. See Carol Lasser and Marlene Merrill, eds., *Friends and Sisters: Letters between Lucy Stone and Antoinette Brown Blackwell, 1846–93* (Urbana: University of Illinois Press, in press.)

3. See Barbara Miller Solomon, *In the Company of Educated Women: A History of Women and Higher Education in America* (New Haven, Conn: Yale University Press, 1985), Table 1, p. 44. Susan G. Broyles and Rosa M. Fernandez, eds., *Education Directory: Colleges and Universities, 1983–84* (Washington, D.C.: National Center for Educational Statistics, 1984), p. xxviii, provides statistics for the academic year 1983–84.

4. Caroline Dall, *The College, the Market and the Court; Or, Woman's Relation to Education, Labor and the Law*, Memorial Edition (Boston: n.p., 1914), p. 8.

5. The most famous opponent of coeducation because of its impact on women's reproductive organs was Edward H. Clarke, *Sex in Education; Or, A*

Fair Chance for the Girls (Boston: James R. Osgood, 1873). See also the essay by
Patricia Palmieri in this volume for further comments on this theme.

6. Quoted in *U.S. News and World Report,* November 11, 1968, p. 63.

7. Quoted in *Newsweek,* January 27, 1969, p. 68; emphasis in original.

8. Mary Wollstonecraft, *A Vindication of the Rights of Woman,* Carol H.
Poston, ed. (New York: W. W. Norton, 1975), p. 117 [originally published
1792]; Wollstonecraft was an outspoken supporter of coeducation.

9. In recent years, Patricia Graham has been perhaps the most visible scholar
to assert the economic motives of those promoting coeducation. See, for example,
Patricia Albjerg Graham, "Expansion and Exclusion: A History of Women in
American Higher Education," *Signs* 3 (1978): 759–73, especially p. 764. The
assertion that economic realities underlie the movement toward coeducation was
not new in the 1960s; Helen R. Olin, *The Women of a State University: An
Illustration of the Working of Coeducation in the Middle West* (New York: G. P.
Putnam's Sons, Knickerbocker Press, 1909), felt compelled to argue that purely
economic motives did not underlie the acceptance of women at the University of
Wisconsin. Thomas Woody's classic work noted that "the reason most often
assigned for coeducation's success was its economy." See Thomas Woody, *A
History of Women's Education in the United States,* 2 vols. (New York: Science
Press, 1929) II: 256ff.

10. Florence Howe discusses these difficulties at length in her title essay,
"Myths of Coeducation," in *Myths of Coeducation: Selected Essays, 1964–1983*
(Bloomington: Indiana University Press, 1984), pp. 206–20; see also her Preface,
ibid., pp. ix-xi.

Because of Oberlin's status as a pioneer in coeducation, many critics have used
it as a test case. Unfortunately, they often confuse bad motives and unfortunate
outcomes. The introduction and essays that constitute the third section of this
volume explore further these questions.

11. M. Elizabeth Tidball, "Perspective on Academic Women and Affirmative
Action," *Educational Record* 54 (1973): 130–35; M. Elizabeth Tidball and Vera
Kistiakowsky, "Baccalaureate Origins of American Scientists and Scholars,"
Science 193 (20 August 1976): 646–52. More recently, some questions have been
raised about these findings. See Mary J. Oates and Susan Williamson, "Women's
Colleges and Women Achievers," *Signs* 3 (1978): 795–806.

12. Virginia Woolf, *Three Guineas* (1938; rpt. San Diego, Calif.: Harcourt
Brace Jovanovich, 1966), pp. 33–34.

13. Adrienne Rich, "Toward a Woman-Centered University," in *On Lies,
Secrets, and Silence: Selected Prose, 1966–1978* (New York: W. W. Norton,
1979), p. 133.

I

Posing the Questions

In the opening essay, "Coeducation in a Gender-Stratified Society," Alice Rossi introduces a range of issues necessary to consider in evaluating the success of coeducation. Observing that sexual equality rarely motivated many formerly single-sex institutions to accept coeducation, Rossi views critically the impact of current trends on the education and the lives of women and men. Applying her analytic tools to contemporary Oberlin College with its long heritage of coeducation and comparing it to the recent coeducational convert, Amherst College, and the single-sex stalwart, Smith College, Rossi investigates how well women students are served in each kind of school. Factors noted include the proportional representation of women among faculty and administrators, as well as "non-college influences" students bring with them. Rossi concludes by identifying the fundamental challenge currently faced by coeducational colleges and universities: "To widen the range of human experiences and knowledge . . . of both men and women."

Coeducation in a Gender-Stratified Society

ALICE S. ROSSI

Over the course of the past two decades coeducation has spread to almost all the most prestigious universities in the United States, and very few private liberal arts colleges that began as single-sex institutions have survived the pressures to become coeducational. Single-sex colleges in 1986 are indeed an endangered species. Many of the hardy women's colleges that have remained single-sex institutions now confront problems of declining applications for admission and requests for transfers to coeducational colleges by their sophomores.

Although men students are now found at Vassar College and women students at Amherst College, a host of questions remain concerning educating men and women together. In particular, three sets of questions concerning coeducation are worth examining:

1. Why have single-sex institutions of higher education become coeducational? What role did concern for women's opportunities and development play in these decisions?

2. What does it mean for an institution to be coeducational? Is a college coeducational if women represent 10 percent or 90 percent of the student body? Is an institution coeducational if there is gender parity among the students, but a faculty that is 80 percent male? Does the curriculum of a coeducational institution differ in any significant way from that of a single-sex college? Does it matter for later adult life whether women attend a single-sex or a coeducational institution, or whether they are taught largely by men as opposed to an equitable mix of both men and women?

11

3. Are there distinctive gender differences, preferences, and disciplinary interests that should inform educators and administrators in higher education? If there are, what should be done about them? Should we try to change them, or should we accommodate to them? Should we, as educators, facilitate the fulfillment of choices that students bring with them when they enter college, or should we attempt to change those choices in keeping with our judgment of the competencies they will need as adults?

TRENDS IN COEDUCATION

For most of American history, private colleges and universities were exclusively male preserves, dedicated to producing clergy and educating the landed gentry. The entering wedge for women in higher education was stimulated by the need for literate women to provide religious instruction for their children, and, once the young nation recognized the desirability of an educated citizenry, by the need for teachers. Coeducation first took hold in public colleges and universities, legitimized by the fact that they were tax-supported by parents of both sons and daughters. By contrast, most private colleges in the latter part of the nineteenth century continued as the producers of male clergy, lawyers, physicians, and political leaders. Advocates of women's abilities and rights to higher learning, rebuffed by the private men's colleges, went on to found parallel single-sex colleges for women. The women's colleges sought to demonstrate that women were capable of benefiting from the same education as men, without endangering either their fertility or psychic stability. Hence their curricula were imitations of those found in private men's colleges. Little wonder, then, that historical precedence was followed in more recent years, as men's colleges admitted women. Because the curricula of women's colleges were similar to those in male single-sex colleges, men's colleges facing the transition to coeducation felt no need to change their curricula, but only to make modest changes in their facilities.

A number of factors have pressed for the more recent transition of so many single-sex colleges to coeducation. By far the most important factor was the threat to the enrollment of private colleges from the great expansion in the size and quality of public institutions of higher education. At the turn of the century, 60 percent of college students were enrolled in private institutions; by 1960 this had dropped to 42 percent;

and by the mid-1980s it was approximately 20 percent. As quality education became available in lower-cost public colleges, the private single-sex institutions tried to increase their drawing power for the dwindling number of high school graduates by becoming coeducational. In 1960 approximately 26 percent of college students attended single-sex institutions; by the mid-1980s fewer than 5 percent attend these institutions, and they are largely at women's colleges. If women's colleges are an endangered species, then men's colleges are all but extinct.

How wide the doors of formerly all-male colleges were opened to women varied a good deal from college to college. When Dartmouth College became coeducational in 1972, 350 women were admitted under a plan that projected a build-up over four years to 1,000 women, while retaining Dartmouth's usual 3,000 men. This three-to-one ratio was thought to be a proper mix, assuring the traditional male emphasis while making concessions to financial need by admitting a minority of women. A sociologist who taught at Dartmouth College during those early years of coeducation reports the college expected to stay exactly the same after coeducation as it had always been; as she put it, "as though women could be planted like trees on the green and nothing would change." But Dartmouth women students soon showed a self-conscious discontent with their minority status, and beginning with the class of 1984, men and women were no longer treated differently in the admission process. One might call this shift to coeducation "sex equality on the installment plan."

Columbia College was the last of the Ivy League colleges to turn coeducational when it admitted women for the first time in the fall of 1983. That it did so despite the presence of Barnard College on Morningside Heights demonstrates the primary motivation of most single-sex institutions that shifted to coeducation. Neither an ideology of sex equality nor the pedagogic desirability of educating men and women together played a role in this decision; economics and demography dictated the changes. Escalating costs coupled with reduced federal funds for financial aid to both students and institutions provide the economics. The shrinking size of high school graduate pools provides the demographics: the size of the 18- to 24-year-old cohort will decline by 23 percent over the next fifteen years, picking up again only in the first decade of the next century.[1] Estimates of declines in college enrollment in the coming decade vary: the Carnegie Council on Policy Studies in Higher Education forecasts a 5 to 15 percent decline in full-time enrollments, and S. P.

Dresch and A. L. Waldenberg[2] forecast a cumulative decline of 15 to 25 percent in undergraduate enrollment by the mid-1990s. It should be noted, however, that these predictions are not uniform across the nation: F. Crossland[3] predicts the sharpest declines will be in a sweep of northern states from Minnesota to Connecticut, whereas colleges in the Southwest may experience continued enrollment growth.

At Columbia College, competition had been keen throughout the late 1970s for the dwindling pool of bright young men from affluent families. The sudden turnabout of the Columbia College faculty from resisting to supporting the decision to become coeducational was rooted in their classroom experience with the lowering scholastic aptitude of the students they taught. The new dean of the college, Robert Pollack, provided a surprisingly frank assessment in an interview: "We will have excellent women in the entering class this fall instead of the bottom one-quarter of the all-male classes we've had in recent years."[4] Clearly both administrators and faculty prefer bright women students to male dummies!

There has been wry amusement in observing developments on campuses that are newly absorbing women into their traditionally all-male student bodies. Like a father untutored in child care who suddenly assumes responsibility for precocious and energetic children, previously all-male colleges were unprepared for the new kinds of choices and demands the early cohorts of women students made: pressure to expand the arts and humanities faculty; appeals for women's studies courses; pressure to increase the proportion of women in the student body to ease the stress of minority status for the pioneer cohorts of women students; and, before long, demands for hiring more women faculty and administrators. Most recently, young women faculty and graduate students have been active in support of classified university women personnel who are pressing for pay increases in new union contracts, as for example at Yale University in 1984 and 1985.

That economic and demographic factors are critical in opening male social institutions to women is not a phenomenon unique to higher education. These factors played a critical role in opening doors for women in many occupations in the labor market as well. It would seem that either severe shortages or oversupplies of personnel are conducive to the entry of women. When there was a shortage of manpower, as during World War II, women were suddenly found capable of working with heavy machinery or supervising dozens of employees, in much the way the shortage of affluent bright male students led to the re-discovery that women are capable of benefiting from a Yale or Columbia education. Discrimination against the employment of married women declined in the 1950s not because employers suddenly had a change of heart, but because the demographic pool of young unmarried women available for employment was one-third smaller than normal as a consequence of higher school-attendance rates, an earlier age at marriage, and a smaller birth cohort reaching maturity (reflecting the low fertility rate of the 1930s).[5] Because there were three million fewer women available who met employers' preferences for young unmarried women employees, the market opened to older, and married, women. Conditions of market surplus or saturation stimulate a similar process: women are earning law degrees and Ph.D.s in the humanities and the social sciences at higher rates than ever before in American history, but they face saturated markets for people holding such degrees, while men have been moving into more lucrative fields like electronics, business management, and polymer science.

Although financial and demographic considerations played a primary role in the trend toward coeducation, there were supplementary factors that also pressed and that help to explain the striking contrast between the very great change in student social and residential life on college campuses and the very slight or nonexistent change in academic curricula or faculty composition. When private colleges were first founded in idyllic rural isolation, the students were essentially pubescent or early adolescent children in need of close supervision. But a seventeen-year-old of a century ago has an equivalent today in a spunky thirteen-year-old. In the past, sexual maturation peaked during the high school years, whereas today sexual maturation takes place while most young people are in elementary and junior high school. Hence by the time students reach college age, they have had many years of sexual maturity behind them and have largely attended coeducational public high schools. The sharp drop in age at first sexual experience was the natural consequence of the earlier drop in age of physiological maturation. By the 1970s college students found it increasingly unacceptable to live and study under conditions of sexual segregation.

Sexual standards have indeed changed, not only in the age of sexual initiation, but in female expectations of sexual gratification and prefer- ences for where and when sexual encounters take place. Quickie couplings in the back seat of a car on a weekend date are largely passé. Young people desire privacy and spontaneity, with sexual intimacy a part of their daily lives. Colleges have accommodated to these preferences by relaxing or abandoning parietal rules, establishing coed dormitories, and providing health services that include contraceptive counseling and referrals in case of contraceptive failure. An adventure of the mind is as central to a college experience today as in the past. What is new is that the college setting now embraces adventures of the flesh as well.

Sadly, the college curriculum has yet to reflect these changes. Despite a mushrooming of scientific research on human sexuality from the neurosciences, reproductive biology, and the behavioral sciences, and despite the clear centrality of sex in the lives of students, one rarely finds a single, full-credit course on human sexuality in the college curriculum. Even where courses are offered, they tend to be electives that earn few credits, or they are but workshops for informal discussions in a dormitory setting. In either event, the silent message seems to be that the faculty does not consider the topic worthy of serious academic attention.

It is here that we must confront two hard truths about higher education: our colleges have accommodated to the *sexual* revolution of the twentieth century through significant changes in the social and residential sides of campus life, but hardly at all on the curricular side of the college experience. Second, our colleges have barely begun to accommodate to the *gender* revolution taking place in contemporary western societies. Like the occasional course in human sexuality, colleges may offer a few women's studies courses, often against the latent if not overtly expressed opposition of the faculty, while the mainstream curriculum remains relatively untouched by new research on gender across a wide range of disciplines. It is to the implications of this gender revolution that we now turn, guided at the start by the question of what it means to label an institution as coeducational.

COEDUCATION AND GENDER STRATIFICATION

The social sciences have learned a great deal over the past several decades about the social and psychological impact of minority status upon minority group members. Ethnic and racial minority groups often internalize images of themselves held by the majority group, a process sadly symbolized in the years before the Civil Rights movement by the tendency of blacks to lighten skin color in family photographs or to straighten hair. Such self-image distortion was often accompanied by lowered self-confidence and esteem, heightened anxiety, and psychosomatic illness.

It has been less customary to see a parallel phenomenon when women represent a small minority in an otherwise largely male social or occupational world, whether in corporate executive suites, Congress, or an academic campus. Studies of women students in the early years of coeducation at Yale, Dartmouth, and Princeton report with some surprise an elevation of stress, lower self-confidence, and lack of assertion in classrooms by women compared to men students. It has been widely assumed that an increased proportion of women in the student body would alleviate these stress indicators. This is a dubious assumption given that many institutions with equitable sex ratios in their student bodies report similar gender differences: some hesitance among women to pursue honors work, a lack of assertiveness in classrooms compared to men, and self-doubt concerning ability to master quantitative skills. This gender contrast was well caught by a faculty member at Oberlin College who reported that she had women students who were very bright but did not perceive themselves to be special in any way, while men students of only moderate capabilities were convinced that their brilliance was going unrecognized.[6]

Gender composition of the student body is only one dimension of the social system a college represents. Another important dimension is the gender composition of the faculty and administration, who hold the power of institutional decision-making and who are presumed to represent important role models for students. It is the faculty who must teach, coax, criticize, evaluate, and grade the student. What messages come through to students concerning the relation between gender and power in most of our liberal arts colleges, and what impact do these signals have on women and men students?

It comes as no surprise that when women were absorbed into the Yale or Dartmouth communities, their exposure was to an overwhelmingly masculine world in which all but a few of their professors were men. But what of our coeducational colleges of long standing? If there has been any long tradition of commitment to equal opportunity for women and a sensitivity to the powerful models of intellect and scholarship a faculty can provide to its students, one might expect to find a high proportion of women at all ranks of the faculty at coeducational institutions. So, too, one would expect women's colleges to be outstanding in providing their students with female role models by having a predominance of women on their faculties.

To provide some concrete data that speak to gender stratification in higher education, I have compared the rank distribution of men and women faculty members at three colleges. The first is Oberlin College, which holds the distinction of being the first private coeducational college in the history of American higher education. The second is Smith College, a women's college of long standing; and the third is Amherst College, a men's college that first admitted women to the entering freshmen class in 1976.[7] All three institutions are small, private, liberal arts colleges in small-town settings. Classification of the faculty by gender was based on a first-name coding procedure, using the 1982-83 catalogs from the three colleges.[8] In the 1982–83 academic year, half of the students at Oberlin College were women; the entire student body at Smith were women; and only a small minority at Amherst were women. If gender equity and the provision of same-sex models had been a concern of the institutions, one might expect some parity by gender on the Oberlin faculty, a predominance of women on the Smith faculty, and a small representation of women on the Amherst faculty.

The results of this analysis are shown in Tables 1 and 2. In the 1982–83 academic year, the Amherst College faculty was 17 percent women, Oberlin College 23 percent, and Smith College 40 percent.[9] It is hardly surprising that women were poorly represented on the Amherst

Table 1. Women on the faculties of Amherst, Oberlin, and Smith Colleges, 1982–83

Rank	Amherst		Oberlin		Smith	
	(recent coed)		(coed)		(women)	
	%	N[a]	%	N	%	N
Full professor	3.5	86	4.3	69	22.6	106
Associate professor	11.9	42	21.1	56	38.3	81
Assistant professor	36.2	58	41.2	51	50.7	75
Instructor	—	3	40.0	20	62.5	32
Lecturer	—	0	30.0	10	44.7	76
Total	16.8	189	22.8	206	39.7	370

Source: Hand tallies from college catalogs for 1982–83 from the three institutions.
[a]N = total number of women faculty at each rank.

Table 2. Rank distribution of men and women faculty at Amherst, Oberlin, and Smith Colleges: 1982–83 (in percent)

Rank	Amherst		Oberlin		Smith	
	Men	Women	Men	Women	Men	Women
Full professor	52.9	9.4	41.5	6.4	36.8	16.3
Associate professor	23.5	15.6	27.6	25.5	22.4	21.1
Assistant professor	23.5	65.6	18.9	44.7	16.6	25.8
Instructor	—	9.4	7.5	17.0	5.4	13.6
Lecturer	—	—	4.4	6.4	18.8	23.1
N	157	32	159	47	223	147

Source: Hand tallies from college catalogs for 1982–83.

faculty, since its transition from a men's college to a coeducational institution was quite recent. Were Smith College the institutional counterpart to Amherst as a historically single-sex institution, one might expect its faculty to be approximately 80 percent female. This was clearly not the case in 1983. Oberlin, with half its students women, had a quite poor profile of female representation on the faculty, only one in five.

Furthermore, faculty women were not distributed in anything like the rank distribution of men at any of the three colleges. At Oberlin, only 4 percent of the full professors were women in 1983, while the proportion was greater, as one moved down the ranks, to 21 percent of the associate and 41 percent of the assistant professors. The comparable figures for Smith College were 23, 38, and 51 percent women as one moved down the professorial ranks, with a similar profile of gender stratification at Amherst College, where 4 percent of full professors but 36 percent of assistant professors were women. With a history of only seven years of coeducation, Amherst College in 1983 was rapidly approximating the faculty rank distribution of Oberlin College, with its history of 150 years of coeducation.

The paucity of women in the upper professorial ranks has important social and psychological implications for women students and women faculty. A closer inspection of the departmental distribution of women faculty at Oberlin compared to Smith College tells us something about the experience of junior and senior women students when they are concentrating on their majors. At Smith College, women chair six of the twenty-four departments, and only one small department (geology) has no woman in the assistant professor or higher rank. At Oberlin College,

only one in twenty-four departments is chaired by a woman. Eight
Oberlin departments did not have a single woman on the faculty in 1983;
eight others had only one woman above the instructor level. In only
one-third of the departments would a woman student encounter more
than one woman faculty member in her major.

Private colleges take pride in having a low student-to-faculty ratio, and
it is true that for the three colleges in this analysis, the overall ratio was
ten students per faculty member. But if there is some advantage to having
access to same-sex faculty members, then the profile looks quite different. At Oberlin these ratios are roughly twenty-one women students for
each woman faculty member, compared to six men students for each
male faculty member. At Smith College, men faculty have no male
students of course, so the sex ratio is seventeen women students for each
woman faculty member. One wonders if this differential, implying a
distinct difference in the amount of time devoted to student counseling
and in the personal demands placed on the faculty, is taken into account
in evaluating faculty, and whether the imbalance in student-to-faculty
ratios by gender has contributed to the inverse relation between rank and
gender. In other words, do junior faculty women carry a disproportionately heavy load of student counseling, to their disadvantage in terms of
scholarly productivity and hence promotion to senior ranks?

It is also important to view the immediate world of a department from
the perspective of a woman faculty member, who is so often not only the
only woman but also has the lowest status in her department. Is there
sensitivity and commitment on the part of the senior faculty to welcome
her and to provide help and encouragement in light of the very heavy
teaching schedules and advising duties a young instructor carries? Does
the department protect her from excessive college committee assignments? The 1980 Oberlin report on women at the college suggests many
women faculty feel lonely, socially isolated, sometimes unappreciated,
and often overburdened with committee assignments. Examples are
given that are familiar to women in the lower ranks in the largely male
corporate world as well as academe, such as proposing an idea that is not
recognized one day, only to hear a senior male colleague put it forth as
his own a week later. Claiming someone else's ideas as one's own is
typically an unconscious process, but it is nonetheless a latent prerogative
of high-status incumbents vis-à-vis lower-status persons, a pattern familiar to many wives, laboratory assistants, and junior management personnel. A monthly sherry party for junior faculty women may provide a

bit of support to counter the social and intellectual isolation, but it cannot compensate for the pervasive impact of working in a gender-stratified social system.

Recruitment and retention of faculty over the years requires local access to data and observation. Hence an outside analyst can only glean partial insight from the institutional data available. There is some hint in the Oberlin status-of-women report that turnover is higher among women faculty than among men. But there has been an upturn in the hiring of women in recent years. This can be illustrated with data on the year of first appointment to Oberlin: the proportion of women among those who were first appointed before 1960 was only 12 percent, followed by a steady increase to a peak in the late 1970s, when 41 percent of the first appointments were to women. (See Table 3.) Some slippage has occurred in more recent appointments, down in 1980–82 to 32 percent from the peak of 41 percent in the late 1970s. Nevertheless, one-third is still a considerable improvement over the 12 percent before 1960.

The increase in the appointment of women to the faculty displayed at Oberlin in the 1970s is not unique, although the regression of more recent years is unusual. Smith College, a longstanding women's college, has shown increased hiring of women in recent years. At Smith, as at Amherst and Oberlin, the recency of female appointments is reflected in the concentration of women in the lower ranks. Some part of this national trend reflects pressure to conform to affirmative action requirements. Still another factor has been local campus efforts to educate the community about the importance of providing women students with same-sex role models. The claim has been that women students need

Table 3. Percentage and number of women on Oberlin faculty according to year of first appointment

Year	Percentage Women	Number of Women
1980–82	31.7	41
1975–79	41.0	39
1970–74	24.3	37
1960–69	12.2	57
Before 1960	11.5	26

Source: Oberlin College Catalog, 1982–83.

women faculty in their majors to encourage the students to aim high and
to persist in studies that will provide entry to significant professional
careers. If this is so, then women should be a small proportion of those
going on to fields for which the feeder undergraduate major departments
included few or no women.

We can test such an assumption with data from an Oberlin report on
the post-college outcomes in professional and personal life of the class of
1972, who were surveyed five years later in 1977. Clearly these were
students whose college years preceded the increased infusion of women
into the ranks of the faculty. My analysis of these data focused on gender
differences in personal and professional outcomes, with several interesting results. For one, there is no suggestion that exposure to a predominantly male faculty depressed the aspirations of Oberlin women
students for advanced study. Although a larger proportion of male than
female graduates proceeded directly to graduate schools in the fall after
graduation (44 percent of men vs. 35 percent of women), by five years
after graduation, there was no gender difference: 76 percent of the men
and 79 percent of the women had undertaken advanced study after
leaving college.

Field choice is quite another matter. The Oberlin data mirror the
pattern on a national level: Oberlin women are heavily overrepresented
in some fields, underrepresented in others. At one extreme, 91 percent of
those who went into library science are women, as are 75 percent of the
graduates who took work in education and the arts, while at the opposite
extreme, only 21 percent of those studying theology were women, followed by approximately 33 percent among those headed for law and
business administration. (See Table 4.) Interestingly, 42 percent of those
from the class of 1972 in the sciences and mathematics were women, and
41 percent of those headed for medicine were women.[10] Same-sex role
models in college can hardly explain these high proportions of women
among the physicians and scientists, since most of the departments
involved in pre-med and science preparation had no women or only one
woman on their staffs.

There is a humbling message in these data: faculty and administrators
in higher education tend to overestimate their personal and institutional
influence on students. Precisely because they are still free from the press
of adult responsibilities, college-age men and women are more suscep-
tible to historical currents and new ideas. Indeed, the prolonged period of
the life course that Americans now spend unattached, free of family and

Table 4. Percentage of women among Oberlin graduates from class of 1972 who went on to advanced study by 1977, according to professional field

Professional Field	Percentage Women	Number
Library science	90.9	11
Arts	77.8	18
Education	72.2	54
Helping professions	56.4	39
Design	53.3	15
Music/dance	50.0	14
Humanities	47.8	46
TOTAL GRADUATING CLASS	47.4	538
Sciences & mathematics	42.4	59
Medicine	41.3	46
Social sciences	36.8	68
Law	35.3	56
Business administration	31.1	16
Theology	21.4	14

Source: Oberlin College, *Report on Class of 1972* (Oberlin, Ohio, April 6, 1978).

job responsibilities, facilitates rapid rates of social and political change in the society at large. Higher levels of educational attainment and hence longer years in school, higher rates of postgraduate education, independent residence, and marital postponement carve out a full decade as unattached adults for increasing numbers of young people. Indeed, the Oberlin report on the class of 1972 shows that *half* the graduates were still single by five years after graduation, and this was as true for women as for men, a marked contrast from earlier social trends among college-educated women, who often dropped out of college while their young husbands went on for graduate and professional training. It is dubious whether college influences played any role in effecting these changes in the timing of major life events between successive cohorts of college women and men.

The message here is that many non-educational influences are at work among young people: family, peers, the media, job experiences, and political participation. These non-college influences may reinforce, dampen, or run counter to the education the college considers formative in the development of its students. The significant social and psycholog-ical yeast pressing for changed views toward gender roles has been at work in young people before the issues find their way into a college curriculum. In other words the college may *lag* rather than *lead* the way toward fundamental changes in life patterns and the belief systems of students. An interesting example of non-school influence on cognitive development can be seen in Barbara Heyns's research.[11] Heyns found that school influence on students' learning is high during the school year, but family influence is at its peak during the summer months when schools are closed. The result is that middle-class students show an increment in learning over the summer months, whereas lower-class students fall behind.

In the same way, college educators might entertain the possibility that the tendency of women students to be less assertive and competitive than men students, and women's relative lack of marked improvement in this respect over the course of the college years, may not reflect a failure of the college to assist women's development but rather differential experi-ences of men and women while they are away from campus. Men students are far more likely to spend a summer traveling alone in Europe, working on a road construction crew, or climbing a mountain in the Himalayas than women are. These are all experiences that can contribute to independence, physical strength, and self-confidence to a far greater extent than the more typical summer experiences of women as camp counselors, interns in social agencies, or students attending summer sessions.

It is also humbling to realize how firmly set many students are at the point of entry into college, again with implications for the professional fields they select. A closer inspection of the specific social and natural sciences Oberlin graduates of 1972 selected underlines this point: physics and economics are predominantly chosen by men, whereas biology and history are strong magnets to women. There is a suggestion here that it is the calculus-based fields (chemistry, economics, mathematics, physics, psychobiology) in which men are three times as likely to major as women, a profile consistent with the fact that although average verbal SAT scores of Oberlin students do not differ by gender (588 to 590), there is a fifty-point difference in average mathematics SAT scores in favor of men entry-level students (625 vs. 575).

This gender discrepancy in cognitive test results and field choice will become of more rather than less relevance in the decades ahead, as microcomputers, with their associated link to quantitative reasoning, make their way into all sectors of academe, affecting the art historian and librarian along with the chemist and economist. It will be of increasing importance for colleges to provide compensatory training in quantitative reasoning and computer science to redress the gender gap in mathematical competence students show as college freshmen.

In providing such training, however, a college should be prepared for a significant proportion of men seeking it out as well as women, now that quantitative skills are as important in the humanities and softer professional fields as in the sciences and engineering. Indeed, Sheila Tobias, who, at Wesleyan University, developed the first program to reduce "math anxiety," reports that men students showed up at her workshops in greater numbers than women. An institution may therefore find that such programs result in an overall improvement in students' mathematical competence but a retention of gender differences unless special efforts are made to reach women students.

One last result from my reanalysis of Oberlin data is of interest in respecifying the importance of role models in the lives of college students. The Oberlin report included some details on the pattern of marriage, divorce, and family formation during the five years after graduation. The findings suggest the marriages formed by Oberlin women graduates are more fragile than those formed by men. As seen in Table 5, of those who married, 11 percent of the women had already divorced by the time of

Table 5. Divorce among Oberlin graduates of the Class of 1972 by gender and college origins of spouses, 1977 (percent divorced of those ever-married)

College Origins of Spouse	Men		Women	
	%	N[a]	%	N
Oberlin	10.0	50	10.5	57
Non-Oberlin	4.8	62	11.5	61

Source: Oberlin College, *Report on the Class of 1972* (Oberlin, Ohio, April 6, 1978).
[a]N = total ever-married graduates.

the 1977 survey, compared to 6 percent of the men. The data included information on whether or not the spouse was an Oberlin classmate, and Table 5 shows the divorce rate among those who married classmates compared to those who did not. This factor made no difference for the women students, but for the men, the divorce rate for those who married Oberlin women was 10 percent, while it was only 4.8 percent for those who married non-Oberlinian women.

It seems highly likely that a critical factor in this pattern is a gender difference in the level of career aspirations of the spouses of the Oberlin graduates, such that relatively few Oberlin women graduates marry men with less complex and demanding training and early careers to negotiate than their own, whereas by comparison, a larger proportion of Oberlin men marry less ambitious women who do not complicate the early stages of their husbands' careers. It continues to be more difficult for well-educated women to combine career aspiration with marriage than for men to do so. Hence the gender difference in divorce rates may reflect tensions produced by dual training and dual career management for a larger proportion of married Oberlin women graduates than for men graduates.

Small colleges in isolated settings typically have more social contacts between faculty and students than public universities with thousands of undergraduates, which makes the gender-stratified faculty of a small college of particular significance for the adults with whom students have contact outside the classroom. A gender-stratified faculty tends to show much higher marriage rates among men than among women faculty. Thus students are exposed to more wives of male faculty than to husbands of female faculty. The Oberlin catalog does not suggest the college has any number of husband and wife pairs holding academic appointments. Hence the social contacts between students and faculty provide few models of women scholars married to men with demanding professional careers of their own, while these contacts do provide many models of men scholars married to women in traditional family and volunteer roles, or traditional female occupations as teachers, librarians, nurses, or administrative aides. The college environment, then, is communicating a latent message not only about *individual* adult life choices, but *relationship* models in the form of couples, most of whom consist of high-status professional men and relatively traditional wives.

Again, however, we should not overdo the emphasis on role models of a direct sort, for it assumes passive students easily influenced by the attributes of the adults in their environment. The rationale for making every effort to increase the proportion of women on a faculty, particularly at the higher ranks, is not simply to correct the traditional linkage of gender to social power or to compensate for past discrimination against women, but to effect a range of subtle changes in the orientation of senior faculty men toward women. The appointment of a woman to a senior position in the administration or on the faculty provides a model not only for women students but for male faculty and students as well. In my observation, even a single appointment of a woman to a high-status position does more than a dozen junior appointments spread thinly across departments. When senior men interact as *peers* with women of accomplishment, one sees a qualitative difference in tone and style of interaction: a lowering of assumptions of male intellectual superiority, a decline in male conversational overriding of women, and some curbing of the tendency to indulge in detailed play-by-play monologues about a ballgame or fishing trip. After a decade of appointments in the predominantly male faculty world at Chicago, Harvard, and Johns Hopkins, one of my delights in teaching at Goucher College (a women's college in Baltimore) was the experience of being listened to, sought out for advice, and having easy access to many senior and junior women colleagues. At Goucher, where the sexes are distributed equally at all ranks, academic women do not indulge in gossip about decisions being made at some distant seat of power, for they are just as equitably involved in making decisions as their male colleagues.

The bitter facts of economic duress clearly impose a brake on any rapid change in the gender-stratified nature of faculties and administrations in higher education in the coming decade. With declining enrollments on the horizon, most institutions are shortening their terms of appointment and seeking ways to develop non-tenured positions. Since women are overrepresented at these entry points to academe, they have a far more difficult time becoming established as scholars than previous generations experienced in the heyday of the expansion of American higher education.

On the bright side, a high proportion of senior faculty will be retiring during the next decade, providing an opportunity for an imaginative administration to use some proportion of the released funds to reassign academic positions to departments that should be encouraged to grow, and to create a special fund to cover the appointments of women and minority group members. Visiting professorships, made attractive by minimal teaching duties and the availability of furnished homes left temporarily vacant by faculty on leave, could also be used to bring senior academic women to departments that have few women except at the most junior rank. These senior women could have both direct effects upon women students and indirect effects through changes in the orientation of men faculty toward women in general and students in particular.

GENDER DIFFERENCES AND THE COLLEGE CURRICULUM

In an era in which significant changes are taking place in the attitudes and personal aspirations of women, it would be rash to hold to any rigid theory of gender-difference causation. It is fashionable in the social sciences and in feminist theory to assume the differences between the sexes are not innate but largely the products of socialization, and hence amenable to change. This is not the place to develop a counterargument, but we can probably agree that the gender differences we observe in the 1980s are less easily changed than we thought a decade or so ago and will probably be with us for some time to come. In this last section, I argue on a different level: that the curriculum in higher education is premised on a male model of thinking, reflecting psychologically one-sided and socially dangerous assumptions.

If one asked what adult competencies a college seeks to develop and refine in its students, high on the list would be autonomous thinking, clear decision-making, and responsible action, together with subject mastery, work commitment, and professional aspirations for independence and success. We expect our students to stop saying "I feel" in favor of "I think" and to be capable of a logical exposition in support of the ideas and theories they espouse.

Theories of human development give a similar emphasis to human individuation, separation, and autonomy. The milestones of childhood and adolescent development in the psychological literature are markers of increasing separation. Thus, for example, the Eriksonian stages[12] of development (beyond the issue of trust versus mistrust in infancy) are all in the direction of increasing separation: autonomy and initiative in the second stage, industry in middle childhood, identity in puberty and adolescence. So, too, L. Kohlberg's studies of moral development[13] suggest a progression from an early stage, when morality is conceived in interpersonal terms and goodness is equated with helping and pleasing others, to more "advanced" stages, when relationships are subordinated to rules (stage four) and rules give way to universal principles of justice (stages five and six).

It was also unnoticed until recent research on women during the past decade that these theories were developed and tested largely on samples of male subjects. When Kohlberg's stage theory was applied to girls, he found them stuck at stage three, leading him to argue that only when women enter the traditional arenas of male activity would they recognize the inadequacy of their moral perspective and progress like men toward higher stages of moral reasoning by rules and universal principles. Like Piaget before him, Kohlberg found females wanting, with a legal sense far less developed in girls than in boys. In another tradition of research, J. Lever[14] found similar differences in the playground behavior of fifth-graders: she reports that boys quarreled all the time during their games, but never terminated the game because of their squabbles; in fact, boys seemed to enjoy the debates about rules as much as they enjoyed the game itself. By contrast, when girls were faced by the same eruption of disputes, they tended to end the game.

There are echoes here of the observations in recent reports from college campuses of the lesser competitiveness and self-assertion of women than of men. It is far more difficult to get women students to project their voices so they can be heard in a large room than it is to get men students to do so, to say nothing of projecting a strong personality. Some may see in these observations a perpetuation of Matina Horner's "fear of success" as a problem among well-educated women.[15] Some recent research supplements Horner's findings, but in an altered theoretical framework. Carol Gilligan and her associates at Harvard[16] have administered TAT story-telling protocols varying in whether the central characters are in isolated, competitive situations or intimate relational situations. Gilligan reports that women perceive danger and violence in impersonal achievement situations, whereas men perceive danger in and project violence into close personal situations. In other words, as people are brought closer together in the TAT pictures, the images of violence in men's stories increase; as people are set further apart in competitive situations, the violence in the women's stories increases. Intimacy would therefore appear to be threatening to men, competition to women.

After numerous studies using Kohlberg's moral judgment protocols as stimuli, Gilligan concluded that theories of human development have used male lives as the norm and tried to fashion women out of a masculine cloth that simply does not fit, leading to the erroneous view that it is women who are deficient rather than that the theory applied to women was inadequate.[17] Gilligan suggests that women's mode of thinking is contextual and narrative rather than formal, abstract, and linear, and that moral problems for women therefore arise from conflicting responsibilities rather than from competing rights, as they do for men.

This contrast between men and women is exemplified by their responses to a moral dilemma concerning whether or not a poor man who cannot pay for the drugs his wife needs to live is justified in stealing the drugs. Men tend to reason their way out of the dilemma in terms of competing principles and to conclude that the value of human life has priority over the value of property; hence drug stealing is justified because it serves the higher priority value of saving human life. By contrast, women stress the consequences of the man's arrest and imprisonment and argue that the man should negotiate a loan with the druggist or seek contributions from family and community to cover the drug cost rather than to steal.

Thus, retention of intricate human relations, an affiliative response, and solutions that imply interdependence among members of the human community are the marks of moral reasoning in women, rather than the agentic, abstract rules of rights that characterize male moral reasoning. Attachment, empathy, interdependence, and affiliation are stressed by women, whereas competition, independence, separation, and formal rights are stressed by men.[18] These results come not from traditional samples of men and women of an earlier era, but from recent studies of samples of Harvard and Radcliffe students in medical and law school programs. Whatever the origin of these gender differences,[19] they will probably be with us for a long time to come.

But which of these two clusters of human qualities are rewarded in our college programs? The chances are there are innumerable occasions for rewards to flow to those who show independent judgment, competitiveness, self-confidence, an ability to stand up well under pressure, and to make decisions easily—all socially desirable attributes we tend to associate with maleness. What are the opportunities for academic rewards to go to those who are gentle, altruistic, aware of the feelings of others, and able to put the welfare of others above their own—all socially desirable attributes we tend to equate with femaleness? Few would disagree that academe gives little recognition to this latter cluster of characteristics.

Furthermore, J. T. Spence and R. L. Helmreich[20] provide a significant challenge to conventional expectations concerning the correlates of instrumental, masculine qualities and expressive, feminine ones. They depart from previous bipolar models of masculinity and femininity in favor of a dualistic concept and show that when socially desirable attributes of men and women are measured, they vary independently of each other *within each sex.* In other words, the instrumental masculine qualities and the expressive feminine qualities *do not preclude each other in the same person.* Furthermore, it was subjects high on both instrumental and expressive attributes who had the highest levels of self-esteem and self-confidence. I would predict that if our colleges were to penalize men for excessive competitiveness or a lack of affiliative concern for others, they would show the same low levels of esteem and confidence that women do when they are penalized, as they are now, for a lack of competitiveness, possession of affiliative concern for others, and contextual reasoning. The implication here is that women show less self-confidence and more self-doubt in academic contexts because of the disjuncture between what they feel and know to be true from their own experiences in the world and what is valued and rewarded in academe.

One last set of findings from the Spence and Helmreich studies is important for the long-range impact of the college experience upon adult life. Spence and Helmreich administered the masculinity-femininity scales to a group of established scientists, together with measures of their work commitment, subject mastery, and degree of overall competitiveness. Of particular importance was their use of an *external* criterion of scientific productivity: the number of references to their subjects' publications in the Science Citation Index served as their measure of scientific achievement. The scientists high on both the masculinity and femininity scales were the most scientifically productive. Furthermore, Spence and Helmreich found that the highest scientific achievement was among those high in subject mastery and work commitment, but low in competitiveness. This finding suggests why test scores or grade-point averages only predict subsequent grades but not adult job performance or occupational success: high grades may go to those with a zest for competition, but most adult jobs also require skills of persuasion, empathy in interpersonal relations, and cooperation, to temper the negative impact on others of high levels of competitive self-interest.

These findings have significance not only for individual young men and women and their educators, but, at the aggregate level for institutions and society at large as well. Following Bakan's lead, both Block and Spence and Helmreich have argued that the fundamental task of all human beings is to balance agency with affiliation, individual pursuits with collective concern for others.[21] Unchecked by the other, either one is destructive to the individual and to the society at large. David Bakan went so far as to argue that American society has suffered from a long history of "unmitigated agency," forcing itself upon other nations as it has upon the natural environment. It is no exaggeration to claim that unless unmitigated agency is tempered by affiliative concern for others—individuals, classes, nations—such unbridled agency may now trigger annihilation of the human species, if not of the earth itself. The challenge for men, then, is to temper their tendency to self-interest with concern for the welfare of others, and the challenge for women is to develop a sense of an effective, actualized self, not as a substitute for but as a complement to their affiliative concern for others.

By the same token, I take this to be a fundamental challenge to our academic disciplines and to the colleges charged with educating men and women together: to widen the range of human experiences and knowledge from which we build our theories and develop our curricula in a way that encompasses the experiences and qualities of both men and women. In so doing, our theories, our educational programs, and the lives of our men and women students will all be enriched.

NOTES

1. *Three Thousand Futures* (San Francisco: Carnegie Council on Policy Studies in Higher Education, 1980).

2. S. P. Dresch and A. L. Waldenberg, "Academe in the Late Twentieth Century: Disharmony, Discontinuity and Development," presented at the NEH IDES Conference, *Toward a Better Understanding of the Humanities Labor Market: The Role of Economic Analysis and Forecasting* (November 30, 1981).

3. F. Crossland, "Learning to Cope with a Downward Slope," *Change* 18 (August 1981): 20–25.

4. An interview with Dean Robert Pollack conducted by Jack Katz, and reported in a Special Issue of *Columbia: The Magazine of Columbia University* 8 (October 1982): 20–23, 38–39.

5. V. K. Oppenheimer, *The Female Labor Force in the United States: Demographic and Economic Factors Governing Its Growth and Changing Composition* (Berkeley: University of California Press, 1970).

6. P. L. Goldsmid et al., *The Education of Women at Oberlin* (Oberlin, Ohio: Oberlin College, May 1980).

7. Amherst College admitted women as transfer students in 1975, so that some upperclass women were present at the time the first women freshmen arrived in 1976.

8. Gender-ambiguous first names were alternatively coded male and female rather than omitted from the classification of faculty. This procedure was followed with catalog data from all three colleges.

9. Note, too, that the Smith College faculty contains an unusually large number of instructors and lecturers, ranks at which women are particularly well represented. This was a self-conscious effort on the part of the Smith administration to diversify the academic specialties in the curriculum and to infuse more young people into the faculty ranks. Smith is in an optimal position geographically to use this institutional device, since there are three other private colleges (Mount Holyoke, Hampshire, and Amherst) and the University of Massachusetts nearby from which to hire part-time instructors and lecturers from the ranks of both faculty and graduate students.

10. A similar high profile of pre-med and science majors has been characteristic of private women's colleges in the past. Knowing in advance of college entry that there is a long period of training ahead, and that the majority of those training for the fields are men, has served to motivate many women students to attend single-sex colleges, where they do not have to compete with men students for the attention of science faculty members during their rigorous period of study.

11. B. Heyns, *Summer Learning and the Effects of Schooling* (New York: Academic Press, 1978).

12. E. H. Erikson, *Identity: Youth and Crisis* (New York: W. W. Norton, 1968).

13. L. Kohlberg, *The Philosophy of Moral Development* (San Francisco: Harper and Row, 1981).

14. J. Lever, "Sex Differences in the Games Children Play," *Social Problems* 23 (1976): 478–87.

15. M. Horner, "Toward an Understanding of Achievement-Related Conflicts in Women," *Journal of Social Issues* 28 (1972): 157–75.

16. C. Gilligan, "Moral Development in the College Years," in *The Modern American College*, ed. A. Chickering (San Francisco: Jossey-Bass, 1981); and *In a Different Voice: Psychological Theory and Women's Development* (Cambridge, Mass.: Harvard University Press, 1982).

17. For a general overview of the inadequacy of life-span theories for an understanding of women's lives, see A. S. Rossi, "Life-Span Theories and Women's Lives," *Signs: Journal of Women in Culture and Society* 6 (1980): 4–32.

18. Although from a different disciplinary base from Gilligan's in psychology, Noddings, a philosopher, draws a similar contrast with the concepts of an ethic

of caring versus an ethic of principle. Noddings argues that women define themselves in terms of the capacity to care for others, whereas men do not, relying instead on what they take to be some "higher" level of reasoning and judgment. See N. Noddings, *Caring: A Feminine Approach to Ethics and Moral Education* (Berkeley: University of California Press, 1984).

19. I have argued elsewhere that the etiology of the curve of sexual differentiation along the life line goes beyond social and psychological factors to the biological substratum of human development. See A. S. Rossi, "Gender and Parenthood," *American Sociological Review* 49 (February 1984): 1–19.

20. J. T. Spence and R. L. Helmreich, *Masculinity and Femininity: Their Psychological Dimensions, Correlates and Antecedents* (Austin: University of Texas Press, 1978).

21. D. Bakan, *The Duality of Human Existence* (Chicago: Rand McNally, 1966); J. H. Block, "Conceptions of Sex Roles: Some Cross-cultural and Longitudinal Perspectives," *American Psychologist* 28 (1973): 512–26; Spence and Helmreich, *Masculinity and Femininity: Their Psychological Dimensions, Correlates and Antecedents.*

II

What Should a Woman Learn?
A Historical Overview

The essays in this section examine the ideology and reality of women's education in America from the colonial period through the opening decades of the twentieth century. By exploring the public perceptions of the necessity and appropriateness of training women and the steps taken to provide women with what was deemed "proper," Linda Kerber's " 'Nothing Useless or Absurd or Fantastical': The Education of Women in the Early Republic" and Patricia Palmieri's "From Republican Motherhood to Race Suicide: Arguments on the Higher Education of Women in the United States, 1820–1920," set forth the context in which to understand the radical nature of coeducational proposals. Both Kerber and Palmieri point out the resistance to women's education, the difficulties women faced in gaining access to either single-sex or coeducational institutions, and the persistence of the battle to maintain the standards and quality of women's education. Interestingly, both Kerber and Palmieri expose the tensions between providing women with the same educational content as men and adapting the course of studies to more gender-specific aims. While differentiating the education of the sexes permitted women to attain more critical consciousness, it also was used as a tool to reinforce women's inferiority and the gender hierarchy of American society.

"Nothing Useless or Absurd or Fantastical": The Education of Women in the Early Republic

LINDA K. KERBER

"What is noble and of a manly tendency is masculine," Plato writes in *The Laws*, "while that which inclines rather to decorum and sedateness is to be regarded rather as feminine both in law and in discourse."[1] The habit of making sharp distinctions between what is appropriate to men and to women is at least as old as the ancient Greeks. One of the most basic of these distinctions is that between the public sector, where men are thought to actualize themselves, and the private sector, the household, in the context of which women make their moral choices. The Greeks also assumed that the public sector posed the most significant moral challenge, and that it was appropriate that men, not women, respond to this challenge. The separation of spheres is far older than its nineteenth-century expression; the separation of the worlds of men and women had intellectual as well as social implications.

American colonists were refugees from a society we now call "early modern"; a civilization in transition from an oral culture to one based on the written word. At the time of the English Civil War, "more than two-thirds of the men and nine-tenths of the women were so illiterate . . . that they could not write their own names."[2] In this early modern society, education meant learning the skills needed for adult life. These skills were less frequently reading and writing than they were the practical skills of the artisan or housekeeper or farmer. Parents taught their children what they needed to learn; apprenticed boys were taught by masters what they would need to know.

37

As literacy was slowly extended through European society, it was extended in a way that was varied by both class and by gender. It is obvious that the clergy and aristocracy became literate in advance of the lower classes; within each class it was assumed that women were markedly less likely to need to read and to write than their male counterparts. Indeed, as Walter J. Ong has brilliantly explained, the study of Latin served as a "Renaissance Puberty Rite," giving upper-class boys a skill that their social inferiors could not claim and a code that only men of their rank could understand. The study of Latin also marked them off from their own mothers and sisters, who might be literate in the vernacular, but with only occasional exceptions—such as Lady Jane Grey and Queen Elizabeth I—were competent in Latin.[3] One of the results of sending the sons of gentlemen to school was that they were *distanced* from the world of women, separated in an intellectual way from their own female relatives.

In the sixteenth and seventeenth centuries two major developments encouraged wider literacy. The most obvious was the Reformation, which, in all its sectarian variants, encouraged believers to read the Bible. This injunction applied to women, who also assumed part of the task of teaching children the principles of religion and, in turn, to read the Bible. Protestant daughters were thought to need to read, although probably more in the spirit of the ceremonial reading of sacred texts than in the spirit of wide-ranging inquiry. They might, therefore, require only rudimentary reading skills and have little need to know how to write.

While girls were learning to read on a reasonably large scale for the first time, a commercial revolution was encouraging their brothers to learn to write as well as to read. The more closely tied a rural way of life was to commercial society, the more necessary it was for the head of the household to be able to read fluently, to figure accounts, and to sign his name as his bond in commercial transactions. In this context reading and writing were both an emblem of and a means to *power,* testimony to an ability to manipulate others in the culture.[4]

Like the bourgeoisie of the traditional western civilization course, literacy was slowly rising through the early modern period, through, that is, the years of colonial settlement in America. But literacy did not increase at the same rate for each class, nor was it displayed to an equal degree by each sex within each class. There remained what might be called a *literacy gap* between men and women within each social class, a gap that would not be closed for English-speaking people until well into the nineteenth century.

This gap suggests the extent to which women remained frozen in a traditional culture while men moved out into a modern one. In *The Wealth of Nations,* Adam Smith sensitively noticed that there were few institutions in England for the education of women. He suggested that this was because women were not thought to need an education that would pull them outside the home into a world of commerce, politics, and the unpredictable. Boys, he thought, needed to be armed with an education that would provide them with the skills to cope with the public world. Smith wrote: "There is accordingly nothing useless or absurd or fantastical in the common course of their education. They are taught what their parents or guardians judge it necessary or useful for them to learn; and they are taught nothing else."[5] Since everyone thought they knew what a woman was going to grow up to be, she could be trained at home to face that life. It was not anticipated that women would encounter the uncertain and the unexpected, "the absurd or the fantastical." Women were frozen in a pre-modern world while their brothers were prepared for a modern one.

The striking conclusion of recent studies of literacy in America is that the literacy gap closed more rapidly in America than elsewhere in the West. One student of English literacy found, for example, that two-thirds of a national sample of English brides could not sign their own marriage register in 1750 (although probably only one-third of London women were illiterate). Studying signatures on American wills (the colonists did not keep marriage registers), Kenneth Lockridge found that at a time when some 70 percent of New England men could write, only 40 percent of the women could. Although literacy increased markedly in large cities, on the eve of the Revolution the gap remained; women's literacy was likely to be half of men's literacy.[6]

But wills tell us about an elderly segment of society, and few married women made wills. The record of deeds is more useful, although it tells us only about the 80 percent of the population who had some property to buy and sell. Studying deed signing in Windsor, Connecticut, Linda Auwers found that 90 percent of the top 80 percent of the women who were born in the 1740s were able to sign their names on deeds—a marked increase not only over contemporary England but America of one hundred years before, where only 40 percent of the women could sign their names. Studying towns in the upper Connecticut River Valley for the late eighteenth and early nineteenth centuries, William Gilmore recently reported nearly universal male literacy by the 1780s, and 80 percent female literacy for the richest 80 percent of the population.[7]

These figures cannot be generalized to all of America. They are specific to *region:* the South lagged far behind, and as late as 1850 one out of five white women in the South was illiterate.[8] They are also specific to *race:* literacy was much lower among free blacks because they lacked opportunity and institutional support, and of course it was intentionally stifled among slaves. In addition, they are specific to *class:* evidence from deeds means we are learning only about people who have property to dispose of.

Even so, these are extraordinary figures. They perhaps can be explained by the observation that the two major pressures encouraging literacy—the Reformation and the commercial revolution—found less opposition in New England than in Europe. Virtually all denominations encouraged reading by believers; even rural farms were tied into a commercial trading network. It is beginning to seem that New England women in the years of the early republic were the most literate women in western society.

The educational scene of the early republic was volatile. Reading and writing, skills once regarded as those of the powerful, were distributed among women to an unprecedented extent. To varying degrees, the generations of women who lived through the American Revolution and the first years of the early republic were aware that they were living through a strategic moment in the history of the female intellect. They could not help but notice, just as we, reading their correspondence, cannot help but notice. Benjamin Franklin received occasional hesitant and almost illiterate notes from his wife Deborah and his friend Margaret Stevenson, who was his landlady in London—that is, from female contemporaries—but he received fluent letters from his and Deborah's daughter Sarah, and from Stevenson's daughter Polly. Both of the younger women had benefited from the improvements in women's education.[9]

The improvement in female literacy had developed in response to a felt need to read and write (sparked by the Reformation and the commercial revolution); it was promoted by improved facilities for girls' schooling. By the late eighteenth century improved schooling for girls received yet another ally: the political revolution. Believing as they did that republics rested on the virtue of their citizens, revolutionary leaders needed to believe that Americans of subsequent generations would continue to display the moral character that a republic required. The role of guarantor of civic virtue, however, could not be assigned to a particular branch of government. Instead it was hoped that other agencies—churches, schools, families—would fulfill that function. Within families, the crucial role was thought to be the mother's.

This perspective encouraged the vigorous extension of formal facilities for teaching girls. Quakers established coeducational schools. Moravians established pairs of schools for boys and girls. New England schools began to hold summer sessions for girls and younger children. As public monies were allocated to pay female teachers' salaries, the functions of the summer schools were gradually integrated into the year-round public grammar school. Many interesting things might be said about the girls' schools of the early republic: their size, their curricula, their social composition, the extent to which they provided careers open to talented teachers and administrators like Sarah Pierce and Emma Willard, the impact they may have had on notable women of the next generation. But especially notable was the profound ambivalence with which these developments were regarded. They could be welcomed with excitement. They were also met with profound distrust.

The hostility with which educated women were greeted has something in common with the skepticism with which upper classes have traditionally regarded the spread of literacy among the poor, or whites regarded the urge for learning displayed by freed slaves after the Civil War. Approval of new competence was balanced by the fear that new knowledge might make its holders more troublesome. As literate women moved into a male world of print and commerce, they found themselves criticized for transforming the roles that had been theirs by virtue of gender. They encountered a variant of the anti-intellectualism which Richard Hofstadter has identified as a distinctive feature of American life in stressful times,[10] which consisted of the assertion that women did not need learning, for they could not be wise; that women's minds were by their nature attracted to the trivial. This idea can be found in Plato (when he discusses women of his own time); it had retained its vigor down the long centuries, and it received fresh energy in the years of the early republic.

Learned women were traditionally the object of criticism, the butt of bad jokes. The Essex, Massachusetts, *Almanac* offered, as qualifications for a husband, "Well read in the classicks, but no Pedant"; qualifications for a wife: "No Learning, No learning either Ancient or Modern . . . well, but not critically skilled in her own tongue—in spelling a little becoming deficiency. . . ." The Philadelphia *Columbian Magazine* complained that "women of *wit* and *fine reading* are . . . destructive of the peace of the husband. . . . The female pedant, as she imagines herself to have a superior understanding, enlarged by learning, will perpetually provoke you with her own corrections. . . . She watches your words, is fearful of your committing a barbarity in speech. . . . She neglects too much her dress and her person; and with no soft endearments, no fondling agreeablenesses will she condescend to amuse and relax the man just returned from business. Sooner live in a prison . . . than be buckled to a FEMALE WIT . . . who is . . . always . . . forward to convince you of the inferiority of your understanding."[11]

At her worst, the learned woman crossed the boundaries of her sex. Addressing a "Lady, Who Expressed a Desire of Seeing a University Established for Women," a contributor to the *American Museum* warned:

> Deluded maid! Thy claim forego . . .
> Science has, doubtless, powerful charms,
> But then abjure her tempting arms,
> For shoulds't thou feel her first embrace,
> Farewell to ev'ry winning grace
> Farewell to ev'ry pleasing art
> That binds in chains the yielding heart.

The criticism included the specific accusation that learning in a woman was masculine. "If we picture to ourselves," Noah Webster's *American Magazine* suggested, "a woman . . . firm in resolve, unshaken in conduct, unmoved by the delicacies of situation, by the fashions of the times . . . we immediately change the idea of the sex, and . . . we see under the form of a woman the virtues and qualities of a man." "Women of masculine minds," thundered the Boston minister John Sylvester John Gardiner, "have generally masculine manners, and a robustness of person ill calculated to inspire the tender passion."[12]

But if there was distrust, there was also welcome. First, learning in women might be welcomed as a path to an upwardly mobile marriage. The best evidence comes from a graduation skit performed in Greenfield,

Massachusetts, in 1800. Fifteen-year-old Sally Ripley played the part of a girl named Nelly, whose words reflect uncritically the attitudes of her traditional family: "Uncle Tristam says he hates to have girls go to school, it makes them so darn'd uppish & so dread[?] proud that they wont work. . . ." Gradually Nelly is persuaded to admit that educated men speak to educated women with respect. She comes to see schooling as a way to make herself appealing to men who are more refined than "humdrum" farmers. She goes to a dance with the students and finds that she is treated like a lady. "They did not say: come along Nell & here it goes Nell—but shall I have the pleasure to dance with you Miss Nelly . . . they treated me so well that it really made me feel purely." At last she reflects, "If I really thought I could get a nice husband I don't know but I should try to larn" and finally decides: "I'll go to school with all my heart. . . . Well now this beat all, that you should by Arithmetic [increase] the likelihood of being married—I'll learn arithmetic, I will, I will."[13]

Second, learning in women was welcomed as a path to specific competencies. These might be enrichments of what were already understood to be female duties, such as needlework and reading, so as to teach children. Competence always was understood to be specifically *woman's*. It would be a generation before Margaret Fuller could demand that "a being of infinite scope must not be treated with an exclusive view to any one relation" and that the soul must be given free course.[14]

In the early republic, plans for women's education were constrained by notions of what women were. "I think the propriety of circumscribing the education of a female, within such narrow bounds as are frequently assigned, is at least problematic," remarked Judith Sargent Murray. Girls should be taught, she thought, to converse elegantly and correctly, pronounce French, read history, learn some simple geography and astronomy.[15] Perhaps the best known of the proposals for a new female curriculum was prepared by Benjamin Rush; he too prescribed reading, grammar, penmanship, "figures and bookkeeping," geography. He added "the first principles of natural philosophy," vocal music (because it soothed cares and was good for the lungs), but not instrumental music (because, except for the most talented, it seemed to him a waste of valuable time), and history.[16] Rush offered his model curriculum in a speech to the Board of Visitors of the Young Ladies' Academy of Philadelphia. The curriculum of the Young Ladies' Academy (which one of the

Board of Visitors called "abundantly sufficient to complete the female mind") included reading, writing, arithmetic, English grammar, composition, rhetoric, and geography. It did not include the natural philosophy Rush hoped for (although Rush did deliver a dozen lectures on "The Application of the Principles of Natural Philosophy, and Chemistry, to Domestic and Culinary Purposes"); it did not include advanced mathematics or the classics. In Troy, New York, Emma Willard added history, geography, science, and mathematics to the three Rs.[17]

Third, learning might be welcomed for its own sake. One is struck by the hunger of some women for learning, for access not only to skills but to wisdom, and by their expression of resentment at their exclusion from the world of books. "There is no reason," wrote Susannah Rowson, "why we should stop short in the career of knowledge, though it has been asserted by the other sex that the distaff, the needle, together with domestic concerns alone should occupy the time of women . . . when literature and the study of fine arts can be engaged in . . . why may we not attain the goal of perfection as well as the other sex? The human *mind,* whether possessed by man or women, is capable of the highest refinement and most brilliant acquirements."[18]

Finally, and perhaps most significant of all, learning could be welcomed as a route to power and an expression of ambition. In an era in which Jefferson was shocked to find Hamilton acknowledging his hunger for fame frankly and openly, it was the more startling to find Judith Sargent Murray writing, in 1784, that young minds ought to be taught to aspire: "Ambition," she said, "is a noble principle." She urged that girls be taught "to reverence themselves . . . that is, their intellectual eminence," insisting that self-respect and intellectual power went together. She warned against attempts by parents to eliminate pride; properly understood, pride (or "self-complacency") seemed to her a useful defense against false flattery and manipulation by others, especially men.

> Self-estimation, kept within due bounds
> However oddly this assertion sounds,
> May, of the fairest efforts be the root . . .
> May stimulate to most exalted deeds,
> Direct the soul where blooming honor leads.

An anonymous female poet, writing an attack on Alexander Pope, claimed:

> In either sex the appetite's the same
> For love of power is still the love of fame . . .
> . . . power, alike, both males and females love . . .
> In education all the difference lies;
> Women, if taught, would be as learnd and wise
> As haughty man, improved by arts and rules. . . .

"There are some ambitious spirits," wrote Emma Willard comfortably, "who cannot be confined in the household and who need a theatre in which to act. . . ." Instead of being distressed at the possibility of ambition in women, she proposed that they use their energies to establish and direct female influence.[19]

A recurrent theme in these prescriptions for women's education was, as Murray had said, that a woman ought to be taught "to reverence herself." The study of history has had an important role in women's education ever since David Hume in 1741 had commended historical study to his female readers as "an occupation best suited to their sex and education." Hume prescribed history as an antidote to novels, which he believed offered "false representation of mankind." But women harbored some skepticism: in Jane Austen's *Northanger Abbey,* Miss Morland explains why she prefers popular novels to history: "I read it [history] a little as a duty, but it tells me nothing that does not either vex or weary me. The quarrels of popes and kings, with wars or pestilences, in every page; the men all so good for nothing, and hardly any women at all."[20]

If "what a woman should learn" included needlework and cooking, it also included women's history, which linked girls to heroic women of the past and attempted, however hesitantly, to provide for women a place in the civic culture, eroding the antique barriers between the world of men and the world of women. Feminist writers and teachers responded to these demands by compiling lists of accomplished women and anthologies of historical snippets. Women's history as a subject of study in America may be said to have begun with the late eighteenth-century search for a usable past. Compilers of "Ladies Repositories," ladies magazines, and textbooks for girls' schools ransacked their libraries, tumbling historical examples about. They were often heedless of chronology: Charlotte Corday might be paired with Lady Jane Grey, Margaret of Anjou with Catherine of Russia. Not until the antebellum years were there coherent histories of American women available for the female audience. Samuel L. Knapp's *Female Biography* did not appear before

1834; Lydia Maria Child's *Brief History of the Condition of Women* was published in 1835, and Sarah Josepha Hale's *Woman's Record* in 1853. Elizabeth Ellet's great compilation of the activities of women during the Revolution appeared in 1848.[21]

In the years of the early republic educators groped for answers to the question: What should a woman learn? What studies are appropriate for the female mind? In 1956, nearly two centuries later, David Reisman delivered the annual John Dewey Lecture at Bennington, which was then a women's college, and asked similar questions. The title of his talk was "Continuities and Discontinuities in Women's Education." Reading it now, one cannot help but be struck by the extent to which the alternatives that Reisman saw women of his own time struggling with were congruent with those that had been present since the first generation of literate women. The alternatives seemed to be: first, a continuation of what had been learned in the home and could certainly be used in adult life—as Adam Smith had said, NO ABSURDITIES. Against that, Reisman proposed John Dewey's option—an education that would be *discontinuous* with what had come before, that would "put pressure on life," open up new worlds of learning, encourage new ambitions, make room for the problematic and, in Adam Smith's word, the *fantastical*.[22] Nelly, who learned just enough mathematics to raise her value on the marriage market, can serve us as an example of one who chose a continuous education; Judith Sargent Murray, who counseled above all to expect the unexpected, spoke for discontinuity.

The first generation to display reasonably wide literacy among native-born white women grappled with these choices; the alternatives would continue to haunt women and their educators from that day to our own.

NOTES

1. "The Laws," in *The Collected Dialogues of Plato*, ed. Edith Hamilton and Huntington Cairns (Princeton, N.J.: Princeton University Press, 1961), p. 1379 (802e). See also Susan Moller Okin, *Women in Western Political Thought* (Princeton, N.J.: Princeton University Press, 1979), p. 65.

2. David Cressy, *Literacy and the Social Order: Reading and Writing in Tudor and Stuart England* (Cambridge: Cambridge University Press, 1980), p. 2. See also pp. 156, 189.

3. Walter J. Ong, "Latin as a Renaissance Puberty Rite," in *Rhetoric, Romance, and Technology: Studies in the Interaction of Expression and Culture* (Ithaca, N.Y.: Cornell University Press, 1971), pp. 119–24.

4. Lawrence Stone, "Literacy and Education in England, 1640–1900," *Past and Present* 42 (1969): 84.

5. Adam Smith, *An Inquiry into the Nature and Causes of the Wealth of Nations,* ed. Edwin Canaan (New York: Modern Library/Random House, 1937), Book V, chap. 1, Pt. iii, art. 2, 734.

6. Cressy, *Literacy and the Social Order,* pp. 145–47; Kenneth Lockridge, *Literacy in Colonial New England: An Inquiry in the Social Context of Literacy in the Early Modern West* (New York: W. W. Norton, 1974).

7. Linda Auwers, "The Social Meaning of Female Literacy: Windsor, Connecticut, 1660–1775," *Historical Methods Newsletter* 13 (1980): 204–14: William J. Gilmore, "Elementary Literacy on the Eve of the Industrial Revolution: Trends in Rural New England, 1760–1830," *Proceedings of the American Antiquarian Society* 92 (1982): 114–26.

8. Maris Vinovskis and Richard Bernard, "Beyond Catharine Beecher: Female Education in the Antebellum Period," *Signs* 3 (1978): 856–69.

9. See Benjamin Franklin, *The Papers of Benjamin Franklin,* ed. L. W. Labaree et al. (New Haven, Conn.: Yale University Press, 1959), passim.

10. See Richard Hofstadter, *Anti-Intellectualism in American Life* (New York: Alfred A. Knopf, 1969).

11. Harriet Tapley, ed., *Salem Imprints* (Salem, Mass.: Essex Institute, 1927), pp. 32–33; *Columbian Magazine,* June 1797.

12. *American Museum,* February 1788; *New England Palladium* (Boston), September 18, 1801.

13. Journal of Sally Ripley, American Antiquarian Society, Worcester, Mass.; reprinted by permission of the American Antiquarian Society.

14. Margaret Fuller, *Woman in the Nineteenth Century* (New York: W. W. Norton, 1971), p. 96. [originally published 1855]

15. Judith Sargent Murray, *The Gleaner* (Boston, 1798), I: 68.

16. Benjamin Rush, "Thoughts upon Female Education," in *Essays in Education,* ed. Frederick Rudolph (Cambridge, Mass.: Harvard University Press, 1965), pp. 28–34.

17. Anne Firor Scott, "What, Then, Is the American, This New Woman?" *Journal of American History* 65 (1978): 679–703.

18. Susannah Rowson, *Mentoria* (Philadelphia, 1794), Preface.

19. Judith Sargent Murray, "Desultory Thoughts upon the Utility of Encouraging a Degree of Self-Complacency, Especially in Female Bosoms," *Gentlemen and Ladies Town and Country Magazine* (October 1784), 251–52. "On Pope's Characters of Women," by a Lady, *American Museum,* 9 (1792), app. I, 13–15; Emma Willard, *An Address to the Public . . . Proposing a Plan for Improving Female Education* (Middlebury, V., 1819), p. 34.

20. Judith Sargent Murray, *The Gleaner* (Boston, 1798), I: 193; David Hume, "Of the Study of History," in *Philosophical Works of David Hume,* IV (Edin-

burgh: A. Black, 1826), 528–33; Jane Austen, *Northanger Abbey* (London: The Folio Society, 1960), p. 96.

21. For fuller discussion of these points, see Linda K. Kerber, *Women of the Republic: Intellect and Ideology in Revolutionary America* (Chapel Hill: University of North Carolina Press, 1980), chaps. 7 and 8.

22. David Reisman, *Continuities and Discontinuities in Women's Education* (Bennington, Vt.: privately printed, 1956).

From Republican Motherhood to Race Suicide: Arguments on the Higher Education of Women in the United States, 1820–1920

PATRICIA A. PALMIERI

> Why is it, that, whenever anything is done for women in the way of education it is called "an experiment,"—something that is to be long considered, stoutly opposed, grudgingly yielded, and dubiously watched,—while, if the same thing is done for men, its desireableness is assumed as a matter of course, and the thing is done? Thus, when Harvard College was founded, it was not regarded as an experiment, but as an institution. . . . Every subsequent step in the expanding of educational opportunities for young men has gone in the same way. But, when there seems a chance of extending . . . the same collegiate advances to women, I observe that . . . the measure [is spoken of] as an "experiment."
>
> Thomas Wentworth Higginson

Scholars studying American social and intellectual history are just beginning to address the question of why women's higher education has perennially been conceptualized as a revolutionary experiment, as the social critic and reformer Thomas Wentworth Higginson observed in 1881.[1] Before the last decade, American educational history was peripheral to the study of American history. Moreover, educational history was dominated by booster portraits of elite male institutions, usually seen through the eyes of their presidents. The exceptions to the male bias of educational history, Thomas Woody's two-volume *A History of Women's Education in the United States,* written in the late 1920s, and Mabel Newcomer's *A Century of Higher Education for American*

Women, issued in the 1950s, stood alone for many years, although they too demonstrated the conceptual difficulty of studying American women's higher education.[2]

A progressive historian, Woody was interested in "out-groups," in this case women, and chronicled their struggle to gain access to institutions of education created mainly for men. For Woody, access meant success and progress; women, by virtue of being admitted to a formerly male educational bastion, would ultimately achieve intellectual, social, and even political liberation.

Newcomer, a professor of economics at Vassar College, sustained this liberal outlook. Focusing on the women's colleges, she cited their propensity for innovation and noted the high proportion of notable women achievers they produced. For Newcomer, as for Woody, women's entry into higher education was a significant positive marker.

The social and political events of the 1960s, the concomitant rise of a new social history, and the emergence of many more educated, articulate women interested in the status of women gave birth to a revisionist school of women's higher educational history. Aggrieved by the documented discrimination against educated women and angered by the meager victories of even the most educated women in the professions, these social and intellectual historians saw the history of women's education darkly. They began to question the equation of access with progress, arguing that coeducation and even the separate women's colleges reinforced patterns of women's subordination in academe.[3]

At the same time, a vocal chorus of disaffected graduates of the Seven Sisters also lambasted women's education. They wrote popular books like *Peculiar Institutions* and *I'm Radcliffe! Fly Me! The Seven Sisters and the Failure of Women's Education,* books whose titles testify to their authors' disgruntlement.[4]

Beginning in the 1970s, post-revisionist scholars have struggled to shed both booster arguments and dark diatribes. Their concern with women's experiences as students and faculty and their analysis of the development of women's culture within coeducational and single-sex colleges display a new appreciation for the complexity of their subject.[5] To these approaches historians must add another: a focus on arguments for and against women's higher education. Only then can we better understand the interaction between the historical context and real changes in the lives of educated women. Such an examination of the ongoing discussion and its social and intellectual setting will make clear the need to reevaluate the periodization of the history of American women's education in the nineteenth and early twentieth centuries. Moreover, exploration of this realm reveals that in the complex history of women's education there is a central paradox: that success, overwhelming success, triggered as many problems (within the movement and without) as would have total failure.

In what follows I will briefly discuss the arguments covering women's higher education in three significant periods:

1. The Romantic period (1820–60) or, to use Linda Kerber's term, the era of "Republican Motherhood."

2. The Reform era (1860–90), which saw the opening of the women's colleges and a vigorous debate about women's higher education. In this period I find the rise of Respectable Spinsterhood.

3. The Progressive era (1890–1920), in which the first generation of college women began entering the professions, triggering a conservative reaction that I term the "Race Suicide Syndrome."

THE ROMANTIC PERIOD: 1820–60

Historians have documented that Puritan culture was suspicious of women; it classified women as evil. Woman's intellect was also considered inferior to man's, and extensive learning for women was deemed inexpedient and dangerous. In a religiously oriented society, higher education meant the production of ministers; thus males could immediately attend Harvard and Yale with a view toward assuming ministerial roles. Women, locked in a private sphere, were barred from all formal education.[6]

By the 1820s a major shift had occurred in women's roles in American culture. Post-revolutionary American society was permeated with an optimism about individuals derived from two sources: liberal enlightenment thinking and romanticism. Rather than stressing women's evil nature, the new ideology elevated and idealized women's capacity to be pure, moral, and sentimental. What impact did this new cultural definition of women have on women's education? In "The Cult of True Womanhood" and other essays, the historian Barbara Welter argues that the romantic image of woman was anti-intellectual. A woman was supposed to be passive, to indulge in domesticity, and to lead a circumscribed intellectual life. Innocence and emotionalism reigned to the detriment of intellect. The virtuous female was thought to be threatened by too much education.[7]

However, it is clear that this same romantic image could work on women's behalf. Romanticism put an emphasis on perfectionism. Educational reformers began to pit romantic images of women against the frivolous "ornamental" woman who lacked education and was nothing other than a dilettante.

In *Women of the Republic,* Linda Kerber notes that the new republic, anxiously seeking to produce a virtuous citizenry, assigned women roles as influential caretakers. Although women were not expected to participate in the public domain, they were given access to education and drawn, if only indirectly, into the new republican experiment by their responsibility to educate their sons. In this period, seminaries like Emma Willard's Troy and Mary Lyon's Mount Holyoke opened; the historian Anne Firor Scott finds that Willard's Troy was a seedbed of feminism rather than a citadel of domesticity.[8]

The new romanticism operated on women's behalf in other ways. Romantic ideology, a phenomenon discussed by Susan Conrad in *Perish the Thought,* equated genius with such qualities as intuition, emotional empathy, and insight, qualities preeminently associated with women. By laying claim to special emotional and moral traits, women could cultivate intellectual roles as teachers, translators, and social reformers.[9] Concomitant with these cultural changes, economic factors were also operating to provide a rationale for women's education. By the 1820s, America was becoming increasingly industrialized, and factory work was beginning to replace family production. In New England, at least, young women were not needed as much as before to tend farms; neither were they expected to busy themselves in home crafts or to devote themselves to domestic chores. As men moved into the urban economy or ventured West, they delayed marriage. Sensing these changes, families in the 1840s seem to have engaged in what David Allmendinger calls a "life-planning" strategy which promoted the education of daughters. A seminary education would allow women to teach, add to the family income, and support themselves until they entered marriage.[10] The common-school movement, with its demand for a cheap labor pool, dovetailed nicely with other social and economic changes that encouraged, indeed forced, women to become educated for teaching roles in the public sphere.[11]

THE ERA OF REFORM: 1860–90

Thus far historians studying women's history in general and educational history in particular have concentrated their attention on the pre–Civil War era. Our understanding of the links between the Civil War and the growing demand for women's higher education are thus minimal. In general we know that war causes disruption in social values and also allows some crossover in sex roles. Moreover, in wartime women often are allowed access to careers because their skills are in demand. During the Civil War, for example, women figured more prominently in public activities such as nursing. We also know that contemporaries believed that a superfluity of single women existed in New England as a result of the war. Addressing Mount Holyoke graduates in 1873, William Tyler claimed that there were 30,000 more young women than men in the region; he thus welcomed the opening of colleges for women. Vassar's president, John Raymond, spoke in 1870 on the "Demand of the Age for the Liberal Education of Women and How It Should Be Met." He declared that "statistics in our time place it beyond a peradventure that multitudes of women must remain unmarried." Moreover, Raymond sounded a new cultural note. He coupled the statistical reality with the conclusion that it would be an "insult to woman" if she had to sit and wait for a man. As he noted, "Under certain circumstances it is good *not* to marry." According to Raymond, it was one of woman's unquestionable rights to serve her country. Hence women, no less than men, should be provided with the kind of education that promoted independent activity and prepared them for work. The Vassar curriculum with its innovations in science training reflected his concern that women be capable of taking their place in an increasingly professionalized society. While Raymond often envisioned women as helpmates in science, rather than as leaders, he still broke with a tradition in stressing that single women had a right to their autonomy and to education.[12] By the 1870s, then, "respectable spinsterhood," not "republican motherhood," was seen as the raison d'être of women's higher education.[13]

Beyond a demographic shift, what had caused such a tremendous transition in arguments for women's higher education? Historians have not pursued this question sufficiently. In 1870, John Raymond astutely connected the movement for women's higher education with the pre–Civil War women's rights movement. He admitted that a vanguard had awakened the public's attention to women's quest for autonomy. While he personally found some of the women's rights leaders to be "vixens and viragos," he noted that "extremists always precede and herald a true reform." Those who followed in the wake of the original agitation might "gather whatever fruit it may have shaken from the tree of truth."[14] To what extent was the opening of women's colleges an attempt to forestall more radical social change? To what extent was this movement part of a larger social reform history? These questions have yet to be sufficiently explored.

In 1868, John M. Greene, in encouraging Sophia Smith to endow a women's college in Massachusetts, stated: "The subject of women's education, woman's rights and privileges, is to be the great step in the progress of our state."[15] In the late nineteenth century, the desire for women's higher education took on the quality of a millennial-like reform movement, not unlike other communitarian reforms that dotted the American landscape in the pre–Civil War era.[16] Conventionally, most social historians conclude that the post–Civil War era was a kind of dark ages, bereft of social reform or behavior. Ronald Walters, for example, concludes that the reform impulse had entirely spent itself by the 1870s. Moreover, to many the Gilded Age has been, in the words of Geoffrey Blodgett, "a vast gray zone of American history, monotonous and inconclusive, an era of evasion, avoidance and postponement, . . . one sterile of purposes."[17]

This standard interpretation is based on a tainted vision of politics in the post–Civil War era and on a paucity of studies in cultural and social history. Women's history and social history are just beginning to challenge this stereotype. The movement for women's higher education must be seen as an extension of the romantic and evangelical reform tradition. It was also an effort to achieve women's equality. Hence, those historians who have focused narrowly upon the history of the organized suffrage movement and view the 1870s and 1880s as the doldrums also miss the import of the social movement for women's higher education.[18]

Indeed, by the 1870s the debate about women's educability had become, at least in middle-class American society, what the abolitionist debate was before it and the suffrage debate after it—a large-scale movement, amorphous, with different intellectual strands, involving the energies of many middle-class women and men. Vassar president John Raymond alluded to this movement when asserting that "the whole world is astir with a sense of the coming change."[19]

Like those other organized movements, the movement for women's higher education had its "antis," in particular a set of doctors and educators who continuously unleashed fears about the deleterious effects on women's biological and social roles. The ideology of the anti-movement, like the ideology of the movement for women's higher education, deserves serious attention, which it has not received from scholars as yet. Most historians cite as the chief malefactor Dr. Edward Clarke of Harvard University, who in 1873 published *Sex in Education: A Fair Chance for the Girls,* in which he argued that higher education would damage women's health and ultimately inhibit their reproductive capacity. Clarke's book caused quite a stir; within a year it went through twelve printings.[20]

Clarke's book and the ensuing controversy are commonly cited by historians of higher education as illustrative of the negative climate surrounding the founding of the women's colleges in the 1870s and 1880s. Historians suggest that as a result, many of these women's institutions became defensive; they compromised their lofty educational ideals and succumbed to genteel domesticity, health regimes, and upholding rather than revolutionizing the cultural norms of "true womanhood."[21] This is, I think, misleading. Clarke's book stimulated a debate which if anything only heightened the revolutionary quality of the struggle for women's higher education. M. Carey Thomas recalled that as a young girl she was "haunted by the clanging chains of that gloomy little specter, Dr. Edward Clarke's *Sex in Education.*" Alarmed by his rhetoric, the adolescent Thomas encouraged her mother to read his book and was relieved to learn from her that broken-down invalids like those described by Clarke did not really exist. That her mother scorned Clarke's dire predictions and encouraged Thomas in her quest for collegiate training demonstrates important information about women's ambitions in the late nineteenth century and the intergenerational context of women's higher education, and introduces the historical questions of family strategies—the relationship between family culture and women's higher education.[22]

It also made the first generation of women students extraordinarily conscious of their pivotal role in proving to the world that women were men's intellectual equals. As one alumna of Wellesley's class of 1879 recalled: "We were pioneers in the adventure—voyagers in the crusade for the higher education of women—that perilous experiment of the 1870s which all the world was breathlessly watching and which the

prophets were declaring to be so inevitably fatal to the American girls."[23]
Here we return to Higginson's theme of "experiment," for the first
generation of college women confronted the experimental, revolutionary,
and adventuresome quality of women's higher education. While Higginson noted its negative implications—that women always had to prove
themselves to a suspicious male world—there is of course another aspect
to experiment: that daring, bravado, and adventure, that sense of being a
pioneer and of course that desire to uphold extraordinarily high norms.
Subsequent generations of women lost that excitement, and the nature of
women's higher education changed. Clarke's dire predictions did not
dampen the women's college movement. Wellesley and Smith opened in
1875, and others followed soon after.

THE PROGRESSIVE ERA AND THE BACKLASH—THE "RACE SUICIDE SYNDROME": 1890–1920

Most historians view the Progressive era as a period of advance when
college women entered the professions of medicine, law, social work, and
academe. But it was also a period of reaction. This reaction took different
forms and emanated from a variety of groups. In 1908, boasting of the
remarkable success of women's higher education, Bryn Mawr's president, M. Carey Thomas, took note of the changing public perception of
college women: "Our highest hopes are all coming gloriously true. It is
like reading a page of Grimm's fairy tales. The fearsome toads of those
early prophecies are turning into pearls of radiance before our very eyes.
Now women who have been to college are as plentiful as blackberries on
summer hedges."[24] Whereas her generation had been ignominiously
labeled fearsome toads, the new college woman was rapidly becoming a
prized pearl. The pioneer band of college women had been so successful
in weathering the dangerous experiment that in the twentieth century
college attendance for women was not a sacerdotal or strange experience,
but a socially sanctioned endeavor. Vassar professor Elizabeth Hazelton
Haight commented on this success in 1917, stressing that unlike the
"stern pioneer" many women now "wear their learning lightly like a
flower."[25]

But herein lay a paradox and a dilemma. Soon the staunch pioneers,
especially the first generation of academic women at the women's colleges, would be as troubled by their amazing success as they might have
been over their failure. As early as 1900 many of them viewed the rising

tide of more socially acceptable college girls as a grim fairy tale indeed—one that spelled death to the dedication they deemed requisite for the intellectual life and the spread of a disease they termed dilettantism.

If women faculty winced at the price of success within the internal college climate, they would soon find themselves confronted by an even thornier set of problems stemming from the growing popularity of college life. In the words of Mary Cheyney, secretary of the Western Association of Collegiate Alumnae, the "very success of the movement, which amounts to a great revolution affecting one-half the human race, has roused men to resist its progress."[26] Not so surprisingly, the 1900s saw a backlash against the women's colleges. Many male educators and doctors viewed the lengthening lines of candidates in the secondary schools with alarm. They believed the women's colleges were "institutions for the promotion of celibacy," producing a disappearing class of intellectual women who were not marrying and hence were committing race suicide.[27]

In 1908, coincident with Thomas's speech about formerly fearsome toads turning into pearls, G. Stanley Hall, a professor of psychology at Clark University, published an article entitled "The Kind of Women Colleges Produce." In it he lambasted Thomas and other "spinster" presidents and faculty who called upon women to be self-supporting and to uphold in high regard the ideal of scholarship and to train for a definite career. Hall railed: "The ideal of our colleges for young women, especially those whose regimentation is chiefly feminine, is not primarily wifehood and motherhood, but glorified spinsterhood." Women's colleges were, according to Hall, in the hands of misguided feminists."[28]

By 1905, a diffuse but increasingly outspoken group of educators, psychologists, doctors, and journalists had registered their alarm at the low marriage rates of women's college alumnae. Even President Theodore Roosevelt was concerned about celibacy. In a 1905 speech before Congress in which he condemned low marriage rates and the equally scandalous practice of birth control, he popularized the term "race suicide." The incapacity or unwillingness of the Anglo-Saxon race and particularly its highly educated members to marry and reproduce unleashed fears that within a generation or two they would die out. Presumably the leadership of the nation would then be left in the hands of immigrants from Central and Eastern Europe whose fertility was quite high, but whose intellect was deemed inferior.[29]

Viewed from this angle, M. Carey Thomas's statement about toads turning into jewels takes on another meaning: no doubt she hoped to assuage the fears of opponents who continued to relish and rely on the image of the college woman as a peculiar creature. In effect, then, from the very beginning the women faculty at the women's colleges had been battling a psychological war on two fronts: they hoped to challenge the larger culture and to change women's role in society, and in so doing they were engaging in a subversive, radical act. At the same time they wished to maintain the image of women's colleges as reputable and respectable institutions, a difficult task given that they were functioning within an inhospitable social climate for women's higher education and pro-fessionalization.

In this tangled conversation about women's education it is extremely significant that often the first generation of college-educated women who became academics wound up fueling their enemies' arguments. They had built their identities on the ideology of the select few: so long as there were only a token handful of women seeking intellectual careers, a system of special patronage and fatherly advising favorable to their careers had operated. Moreover, the tolerance for the select few meant that only someone like Madame Curie might succeed; faculty women could never settle for being average. They set appallingly high standards for themselves and for their students.

Shocked and dismayed by how few women wanted to follow the scholarly path, some faculty balked at what they called the universaliza-tion of collegiate norms. Average women were getting the B. A. and coming to symbolize the "College Type." But as Margaret Deland astute-ly noted in 1910: "[The] occasional women who did so-called un-womanly things, that is, unusual things generally left to men . . . who have distinguished themselves . . . were conspicuous, because they were strays. Achieving women are not very conspicuous now, simply because there are more of them."[30]

Ironically, then, on one level, proponents and detractors of women's higher education had a mutual investment in the ideology of the select few. For the faculty at the women's colleges, any dilution of the norms or shift from the high standards threatened their status. So long as a raison d'être for college attendance was scholarship and was wrapped up in vows of renunciation, successful academic women appeared irrefutably to be geniuses and would be tolerated. Wary opponents of women's higher education were also satisfied with this equation; they could always explain away or dismiss (even while they praised) the remarkable rare exceptions. But the popularization of collegiate life caused them alarm. They were distraught because more women than they had expected were earning Phi Beta Kappa keys and seeking entry into the professions. However, only rarely did these antifeminists focus directly on their fears of feminization of colleges and professions. In 1901 Hugo Munsterberg, a professor of philosophy at Harvard, voiced his alarm: "In the colleges and universities men still dominate, but soon will not if things are not changed; the great numbers of young women who pass their doctoral examinations and become specialists in science will have more and more to seek university professorships, or else they will have studied in vain. And here, as in the school, the economic conditions strongly favour the woman; since she has no family to support, she can accept a position so much smaller that the man is more and more crowded from the field. And it may be clearly foreseen that, if other social factors do not change, women will enter as competitors in every field where the labour does not require specifically masculine strength. So it has been in the factories, so in the schools and so, in a few decades, it may be in the universities. . . ."

While in 1904 Munsterberg could acknowledge with relief that "professional chairs for the most part belong to men," he still worried over the ultimate feminization of American culture. Any success he attained would be devalued because women had demonstrated equal achievement. "The triumph in . . . competition is no honour if it consists in bidding under the market price. In fact, it is not merely a question of the division of labour, but a fundamental change in the character of the labour."[31] Such fears confirm the argument made by Margaret Rossiter in *Women Scientists in America:* that the growing numbers of women in the professions threatened many academic men who were caught up in defining their career paths as professional rather than amateur.[32] Like other professional men, Munsterberg was anxious to divorce himself from the cheapening effect that feminization has on the status of any profession.

Ultimately, the pioneers would discover that there was a price to be paid for an explanation of college generations that revolved around the fact that a first generation of staunch scholars were, happily or unhappily, passing from the scene. Defenders of the women's colleges were giving their opponents some potent psychological weapons. By 1920, critics and advocates agreed that the experience of the first cohort of college-educated women who went into the professions and who remained single was not representative of normal womanhood. This kind of defense was at one level useful in soothing fears and dismissing doubts about the future status of women's higher education, but it also helped to mythologize the select few, and worse, it labeled them as deviant. Of course the ideology of the select few had always had this vulnerable underbelly—one was intellectually select and prized, but one stood apart and was different from ordinary women.

The negative implications of this "extraordinary woman" approach can be clearly seen in a defense of women's higher education entitled "Education and Fecundity," written by Nellie Seeds Nearing and published in 1914 by the American Statistical Association. She argued that the "average woman . . . who went to college in the early days . . . was not the type who would have been apt to marry in any case." Just who were the pioneers? They "consisted largely of the woman who had some special talent which she wished to develop and practice, the woman of strong intellectual proclivities, who preferred not to engage in the domestic occupations usually relegated to women, and the woman who, because of personal unattractiveness, knew or feared her lack of popularity among men." The contemporary college woman, somehow, was irrefutably different. "Today it is the normal, not the unusual girl who goes to college. . . . It has become a common comfort. . . ." Nearing also believed that a college education had become desirable because it polished off a woman's cultural education.[33]

Mollifying the opponents of women's colleges by emphasizing the conventionality of the collegiate experience for women drew attention away from the fact that marriage rates for college-educated women remained lower than those for the rest of the eligible population. In 1923, Vassar economics professor Mabel Newcomer found that as of the summer of 1922, of 4,424 alumnae surveyed, only 55.6 percent had married. Although Vassar women, she noted, were marrying more, and marrying at younger ages, the total picture was one of deviation from the national averages of marriage rates, which usually hovered around 90 percent.[34] Nellie Nearing had understood this, but she took pains to explain the tremendous disparity by factors other than education. She was led back to economic arguments that noted that educated people expected a high standard of family living and that it was difficult for women to find husbands who could meet this elevated standard.

The constant need to explain away such potent statistics highlights as well the culturally charged climate of the first quarter of the twentieth century, in which marriage and family were deemed by Freudian dicta to be universally desirable experiences craved by all normal women. World War I temporarily masked the shifting social scene that produced hostility toward professional women. Writing in 1938, Marjorie Nicholson, a professor at Columbia University who had received her B. A. in 1914, commented: "We of the pre-war generation used to pride ourselves sentimentally on being the 'lost generation,' used to think that because war cut across the stable path on which our feet were set we were an unfortunate generation. But as I look back upon the records, I find myself wondering whether our generation was not the only generation of women which ever really found itself. We came late enough to escape the self-consciousness and belligerence of the pioneers, to take education and training for granted. We came early enough to take equally for granted professional positions in which we could make full use of our training. This was our double glory. Positions were everywhere open to us; it never occurred to us at that time that we were taken only because men were not available. . . . The millennium had come; it did not occur to us that life could be different. *Within a decade shades of the prison house began to close, not upon the growing boy, but upon the emancipated girls* [emphasis added]".[35]

By the end of the 1920s, renunciation of marriage in favor of professional life was equated with a race of "warped, dry creatures."[36] Reconciliation of marriage and career became the watchword of the 1920s. Educated women "wearing their learning lightly like a flower" attempted to combine career and marriage. But lacking the support of institutions and bereft of a feminist movement, such attempts were often thwarted.

In the 1920s and continuing into the 1930s and 1940s, critics still questioned the value of women's higher education. Detractors insisted that college attendance posed innumerable dilemmas for modern American women. Thus, at some level, higher education for women was still being discussed as an experiment, the view that Higginson had castigated some forty years before. Unwilling to accept the permanency of women's entrance into academia as students or as scholars and unable to accept professional advancement of women in a wide range of careers, critics still dubbed such advances by women as "revolutionary," their worth still to be proved. But despite doubts, American women's entry into and success within higher education permanently altered their life courses and changed as well the social and intellectual course of the nation.

NOTES

1. Thomas Wentworth Higginson, "Experiments," *Common Sense about Women* (Boston: Lee and Shepard, 1882), p. 199.

2. Thomas Woody, *A History of Women's Education in the United States* (New York: Farrar, Straus and Giroux, 1980; originally published by Science Press, 1929); Mabel Newcomer, *A Century of Higher Education for American Women* (New York: Harper and Brothers, 1959).

3. See, for example, Jill Conway, "Perspectives on the History of Women's Education in the United States," *History of Education Quarterly* 14 (Spring 1974): 1–12; P. A. Graham, "So Much to Do: Guides for Historical Research on Women in Higher Education," *Teachers College Record* 75 (February 1975): 421–29; P. A. Graham, "Expansion and Exclusion: A History of Women in American Higher Education," *Signs* 3 (Summer 1978): 759–73.

4. Elizabeth Kendall, *Peculiar Institutions* (New York: G. P. Putnam's Sons, 1975); Liva Baker, *I'm Radcliffe! Fly Me! The Seven Sisters and the Failure of Women's Education* (New York: Macmillan, 1976).

5. For example, see Lynn Gordon, "Coeducation on Two Campuses: Berkeley and Chicago, 1890–1912," in *Women's Being, Woman's Place: Female Identity and Vocation in American History,* ed. Mary Kelly (Boston: G. K. Hall, 1979), 171–94; Patricia Foster Haines, "For Honor and Alma Mater: Perspectives on Coeducation at Cornell University, 1868–1885," *Journal of Education* 159 (August 1977): 25–37; Patricia Ann Palmieri, "Here Was a Fellowship: A Social Portrait of the Academic Community at Wellesley College, 1890–1920," *History of Education Quarterly* 23 (Summer 1983): 195–214.

6. Laurel Thatcher Ulrich, "Vertuous Woman Found: New England Ministerial Literature, 1668–1735," *American Quarterly* 28 (Spring 1976): 19–40.

7. Barbara Welter, "The Cult of True Womanhood" in *Dimity Convictions: The American Woman in the Nineteenth Century* (Athens: Ohio University Press, 1976), pp. 21–41.

8. Linda Kerber, *Women of the Republic: Intellect and Ideology in Revolutionary America* (Chapel Hill: University of North Carolina Press, 1980).

9. Susan Conrad, *Perish the Thought: Intellectual Women in Romantic America, 1830–1860* (Secaucus, N.J.: Citadel Press, 1978).

10. David Allmendiger, "Mount Holyoke Students Encounter the Need for Life Planning, 1837–1850," *History of Education Quarterly* 19 (1979): 27–47.

11. On the common school movement, see Carl F. Kaestle, *Pillars of the Republic: Common Schools and American Society, 1780–1860* (New York: Hill and Wang, 1983). Also see Nancy Hoffman, *Women's True Profession* (New York: Feminist Press, 1981).

12. John Raymond, "The Demand of the Age for the Liberal Education of Women and How It Should Be Met," in *The Liberal Education of Women,* ed. James Orton (New York: A. S. Barnes, 1873), pp. 27–58.

13. For a discussion of the culture of spinsterhood before the Civil War, see Lee Chambers-Schiller, *Liberty, A Better Husband: Single Women in America: The Generations of 1780–1840* (New Haven, Conn.: Yale University Press, 1984); Patricia Ann Palmieri, " 'This Single Life': Respectable Spinsterhood" *American Quarterly* forthcoming (review of Chambers-Schiller, 1984).

14. Raymond, "Demand for Liberal Education," p. 50.

15. John M. Greene to Sophia Smith, January 7, 1868, Smith College Archives.

16. On the reform spirit, see John L. Thomas, "Romantic Reform in America, 1815–1865," *American Quarterly* 17 (Winter 1965): 656–681.

17. Ronald G. Walters, *American Reformers, 1815–1860* (New York: Hill and Wang, 1978). Geoffrey Blodgett, "A New Look at the Gilded Age: Politics in a Cultural Context," in *Victorian America,* ed. Daniel Walker Howe (Philadelphia: University of Pennsylvania Press, 1976).

18. The traditional interpretation that views the 1870s and 1880s as a quiet era can be found in Aileen Kraditor, *The Ideas of the Woman Suffrage Movement, 1880–1920* (Garden City, N. Y.: Doubleday, 1971), p. 4. Recently, some scholars studying women's higher educational history have challenged this conclusion. See Sally Gregory Kohlstedt, "Maria Mitchell: The Advancement of Women in Sciences," *New England Quarterly* 51 (March 1978): 39–63.

19. Raymond, "Demand for Liberal Education," pp. 50–51.

20. Edward Clarke, *Sex in Education or A Fair Chance for the Girls* (Boston: J. R. Osgood, 1874).

21. Sheila Rothman, *Woman's Proper Place* (New York: Basic Books, 1978).

22. M. Carey Thomas, "Present Tendencies in Women's College and University Education," *Educational Review* 25 (1908): 64–85, reprinted in *The Educated Woman in America,* ed. Barbara Cross (New York: Teachers College Press, 1965), p. 162.

23. Louise McCoy North, "Speech for '79 and the Trustees at Semi-Centennial" (Wellesley, Mass.: North Unprocessed Papers, Wellesley College Archives, 1979).

24. Thomas, "Present Tendencies," p. 162; See also Julia Ward Howe, ed.,

Sex and Education: A Reply to Dr. E. H. Clarke's "Sex in Education" (Boston: Roberts Brothers, 1874).

25. Elizabeth Hazelton Haight, "Pleasant Possibles in Lady Professors," *Journal of the Association of Collegiate Alumnae*, 11 (September 1917): 10–17.

26. Mary Cheyney, "Will Nature Eliminate the College Woman?" *Association of Collegiate Alumnae*, 3rd ser., 10 (January 1905): 1–9.

27. William L. Felter, "The Education of Women," *Educational Review* 31 (1906): 360.

28. G. Stanley Hall, "The Kind of Women Colleges Produce," *Appleton's Magazine*, September 1908, p. 314.

29. On race suicide and its relationship to immigration and other cultural issues, see Linda Gordon, *Woman's Body, Woman's Right: A Social History of Birth Control in America* (New York: Grossman, 1976).

30. Margaret Deland, "The Change in the Feminine Ideal," *Atlantic Monthly* 105 (March 1910): 289.

31. Hugo Munsterberg, *The Americans* (New York: McClure, Phillips, 1904), p. 5.

32. Margaret Rossiter, *Women Scientists in America* (Baltimore: Johns Hopkins University Press, 1982) pp. 73–100.

33. Nellie Seeds Nearing, "Education and Fecundity," *American Statistical Association* 14 (June 1914): 156.

34. Mabel Newcomer, "Vital Statistics from Vassar College," *American Journal of Sociology* 29 (July 1923–May 1924): 430–42.

35. Marjorie Hope Nicholson, "The Rights and Privileges Pertaining Thereto," *Journal of the American Association of University Women* 31 (April 1938): 136.

36. Ethel Puffer Howes, "Accepting the Universe," *Atlantic Monthly*, 129 (April 1922): 453.

III

Creating a Coeducational Model: The Historical Meaning of the Oberlin Experience

The third section of this volume reexamines the significance of the unprecedented decision of Oberlin Collegiate Institute to enroll four women in the baccalaureate course in 1837, when no other institution was yet prepared to grant women regular access to study at the collegiate level. Traditionally, historians applauded the enlightenment of Oberlin's founders for including women in their plans. But more recently, revisionists have criticized the institution for providing women access only in order to serve men, to do the domestic labor of the institute or to marry male graduates as well-educated but appropriately subordinate spouses. As Lori Ginzberg points out in her essay, "The 'Joint Education of the Sexes': Oberlin's Original Vision," Oberlin's founders were concerned with the place and role of women in a religious community; that those who countenanced the radical educational experiment did so from motives different from those of twentieth-century feminists can hardly be surprising. They viewed women as morally different from men and conceptualized women's contribution to the community as equitable, but not the same. Still, Oberlin did consciously provide women with "all the instructive privileges which hitherto have unreasonably distinguished the leading sex from theirs," educational tools that ultimately proved revolutionary.[1]

Barbara Miller Solomon's essay, "The Oberlin Model and Its Impact on Other Colleges," demonstrates that the Oberlin model loomed large in the minds of those who subsequently considered bringing coeducation to their campuses. Solomon's work effectively demonstrates how coeducation *has* made a difference by opening the door through which most women in higher education now pass. Janet Giele's "Coeducation or Women's Education: A Comparison of Alumnae from Two Colleges, 1934–1979" compares Oberlin's alumnae to graduates of a Seven Sisters college over the last fifty years and demonstrates that women graduates of Oberlin in this period were in their own times pioneers, leading the way in combining work and family. This pattern, clear in the life histories of Oberlin's alumnae for half a century, is now the experience of the overwhelming majority of American women. Just as Oberlin led the way in providing advanced education to women, so her alumnae have shown the way to new life courses for women.

NOTE

1. The quotation is from a circular for the Oberlin Collegiate Institute issued March 1834, cited in Robert Samuel Fletcher, *A History of Oberlin College from its Foundation through the Civil War,* 2 vols. (Oberlin, Ohio: Oberlin College, 1943), I: 373. Fletcher's is the classic work on Oberlin College; his chapters "Female Reformers" (I: 290–315) and particularly "Joint Education of the Sexes" (1: 373–85) are key sources, widely quoted by those who now find fault with the motives of the founders. For a "revisionist" perspective that offers a more critical appraisal of the achievement of access, see Ronald W. Hogeland, "Coeducation of the Sexes at Oberlin College: A Study of Social Ideas in Mid-nineteenth-century America," *Journal of Social History* 6 (Winter 1972–73): 160–76; and the work of historian Jill Conway, including "Perspectives on the History of Women's Education in the United States," *History of Education Quarterly* 14 (1974): 1–12, and "Coeducation and Women's Studies: Two Approaches to the Question of Woman's Place in the Contemporary University," *Daedelus* 103 (1974): 239–49.

The "Joint Education of the Sexes": Oberlin's Original Vision

LORI D. GINZBERG

Discussions about joint education have traditionally shared a common concern: namely, whether women would—or would not—live "up" to the standards of men. Both proponents and opponents of coeducation have judged its success based on this criterion. Nineteenth-century woman's rights advocates exulted in a new status for the well-educated woman who could think and act on men's level. Opponents of the "joint education of the sexes" asserted, somewhat illogically, both that women were incapable of performing at men's intellectual level and that such performance was socially undesirable; not only would women become "manly," but, according to one critic, coeducation "has tended to produce that contempt of the much vaunted superiority of man that is as a rule reserved for the post nuptial discoveries which make marriage such an interesting venture."[1] The power of this rhetoric becomes clear when one notes the urgency with which coeducation's advocates insisted that educated women would preserve their femininity, would use their education in a manner appropriate to their sex, and, above all, would marry.

As the first school to grant college degrees to both women and men, Oberlin has always figured prominently in this discussion. Recent historians, sympathetic to the goals of female "equality," have faulted Oberlin's experiment in coeducation for not truly placing women on a par with men. Yet the founders themselves neither intended nor expected the intense debate that followed their almost casual inclusion of women in the institute.[2] In their search for conservative elements in the new endeavor, historians have exaggerated the inequalities between Oberlin women's and men's curriculum in the 1830s and have viewed out of context the founders' incorporation of traditional sex roles in the manual labor department of the institute.[3] More important, historians have misdirected their focus on the issue of "equality" itself. This discussion places the history of coeducation at Oberlin in the context of a new understanding of "standards." Those who measure endlessly the extent to which Oberlin women were expected to perform like men miss the radical implications of the Oberlin experiment, and of Oberlin's goals. For Oberlin in the 1830s was not merely an educational institution in any narrow sense; it was a model for the "world's enlightenment and regeneration."[4] The evangelical and domestic world-view of its founders and students demanded less that women perform on men's level than that men live up to the standards of women.

Oberlin's early experience with the joint education of women and men in their shared quest for millennial perfection would leave behind an ambiguous legacy for the coeducational institutions that followed. By exalting "female" qualities and virtues and working to incorporate them into male students, Oberlin's pioneers raised implicitly the question of just what, if anything, was inherent in women and what in the gender identities of women and men could be modified by education and exposure to the other sex. Although many of the schools which followed Oberlin's lead lacked the religious motive that had actuated the founders, they too became embroiled in discussions of gender identities and power relations, the nature of femininity and masculinity, and the extent to which education shaped the social experience of gender itself.

As is by now well known, the 1820s and 1830s were a period of ideological upheaval for evangelical Protestants.[5] The revivals of the Second Great Awakening, which were led by Oberlin's future president, Charles Finney, swept across New England and western New York and left in their wake a generation of women and men who would carry their religious fervor into numerous reform efforts. They believed that human perfection was attainable through individual conversion and submission to God and that the perfectability of each individual implied, indeed demanded, passionate efforts to transform society. Their moral fervor and their revivalistic language spilled over into social causes. As abolitionists, temperance workers, moral reformers, vegetarians, teachers, and members of utopian communities, they sought to purify the world through the rejection of sin by each of its inhabitants individually.

Women were central to both the audience and the ideology of this reform spirit. Evangelical reform fit well with an activist ideology of women's "sphere." Best articulated by Catharine Beecher, this ideology maintained that women's inherent gender characteristics, as well as their social roles as wives, mothers, and, increasingly, teachers, made them peculiarly fit to carry the message of submission, piety, and virtue to the world. According to Beecher, women would forge power from subordination, activism from domesticity, national unity from heightened gender differences.[6]

Their strategy was simple: Christian virtues were, increasingly, defined as inherently—and aggressively—female virtues. Women would teach their sons to be more like themselves, and therefore diffuse the conflict inherent in "masculine" life and in class identity. Reformers called upon women to assert their unique characteristics in transforming the "male sphere."

The interest in Oberlin as a coeducational and interracial college has obscured its significance as a religious community, that is, as an experiment in Christian virtue which grew directly out of the spirit of the Second Great Awakening. When they established the Oberlin community and institute in 1833, Oberlin's founders informed the world that they "lament[ed] the degeneracy of the church and the deplorable condition of our perishing world. . . ."[7] They set out for the frontier to create a model society, one that would demonstrate true Christian living to a slave-holding, Sabbath-breaking, materialistic society. The training of missionaries, teachers, and reformers of both sexes was a central purpose. Equally significant was Oberlin's insistence on applying female virtues to community life. The female model—and therefore women—were essential in the work of transforming society.

James Fairchild, who was at various times student, teacher, and president of Oberlin, argued both that women should be educated as human beings and that they would be a "civilizing influence" on men in "public life."[8] Similarly, Charles Finney believed that women's presence would benefit men; it would free men of sentimentalism and allow them to proceed with their Christian duty. An isolated, all-male society, he felt, distorted reality and gave men romantic images of the "female character." Yet the concept of females' moral superiority did not serve as a pretext for bringing women to Oberlin to serve men, do laundry, and become wives. Oberlin was to be a place where women's supposed moral influence would be strong and where men would learn the qualities that made women capable of changing society. One might expect that, faced with the "stark reality" of female students, the men would lessen their expectations of what Finney termed these "true vehicles of God's grace."[9] Yet Oberlin students and faculty seem to have been unaffected by the contradiction between women as standards of virtue and as real individuals in the community. Instead, these expectations, and the religious fervor of the participants, inspired women at Oberlin to exemplify the (supposedly inherent) standards of their sex.[10]

In any case, the participants in the experiment believed that it worked. In 1836, the faculty and trustees met to discuss joint education. They reported that it cultivated "mind and manners, promote[d] real virtue, and correct[ed] frivolities, irregularities, and follies common to youth."[11] Oberlin congratulated itself on having avoided the riots then taking place in all-male colleges; participants attributed this to the very presence of women. No doubt the type of men Oberlin attracted added to the impression that coeducation created a more pious and orderly environment. But women, who came to Oberlin both for an education and to fulfill a moral mission, made possible one of Oberlin's primary functions: the creation of a society that would show the world the harmony and virtue of Christian living.

Oberlin members went about community-building with the same self-conscious fervor with which they approached all aspects of life, with that "seriousmindedness" which Robert Fletcher, the historian of the college, called "appalling."[12] The experience of belonging to the Oberlin community was intense. Letters between women students and teachers frequently expressed affection for one another, for Oberlin, and for its "privileges." Upon arriving at Oberlin in 1837, Nancy Prudden remarked, "The sisters all seem to love one another and of course are happy." Ann Elisa Gillett left Oberlin with reluctance because she would miss her acquaintances of the two most pleasant years of her life. At Oberlin, she recalled, "All is peace, love, harmony and good will."[13] Many Oberlin women married men who shared their intense commitment to values fostered at Oberlin; other students, like Sallie Holley and Caroline Putnam, formed with each other relationships that would last through a lifetime of reform activity.[14] From voting on rules in Ladies' Hall, to organizing anti-slavery, literary, and moral reform societies, to performing manual labor, the Oberlin experience created for women a model that they would take with them when they left. It gave them a glimpse of a community in which women's values and women's work were essential elements of its success.

Early Oberlin has frequently been faulted for its manual labor system, with its clear sexual division of labor. That criticism needs to be not fully withdrawn but mediated by a more subtle understanding of the role of the division of labor in the model community. Generally women did sewing, laundry (for themselves as well as for the men), and prepared and served meals. They did not attend classes on Monday, devoting the day to laundry. They attended numerous lectures by Alice Cowles, the "ladies' principal," on how to make collective domestic labor more scientific. Significantly, women were paid for their work. Robert Fletcher estimated that, in 1836, 60 percent of women's total expenses were paid for by domestic labor; the "economic relation between the sexes," he wrote, "was much the same as that in any well-regulated family."[15] Advocates of the system emphasized both the mutual economic dependence between women and men and the effort to perpetuate a stable community based on so-called family functions.

In practice, however, these functions were not entirely rigid. The male editors of *Oberliniana* recalled that one of them had mopped floors in Ladies' Hall as part of his manual labor duties.[16] Another was, apparently for some time, a waiter in the dining room. Frequently critical of Oberlin's inequalities, Lucy Stone nevertheless described the manual labor system as rather flexible: "Future governors of the State, members of Congress, generals of armies, were part of the working brigade of Oberlin. General [Jacob Dolson] Cox, with paper cap on his head, with apron and sleeves rolled up, made the crackers which, on Sunday mornings, with coffee, made the breakfast."[17] Apparently, for men at Oberlin, who sought to build a society that embodied "female values," it was not unknown to participate in "female" work.

In more explicit ways as well, men at Oberlin sought to adopt women's standards for their own behavior. In 1835 both a female and a male moral reform society were formed in Oberlin, auxiliary to the New York Female Moral Reform Society. It was in the NYFMRS that Beecher's ideal of a "national ethic of domestic virtue"[18] reached its most aggressive form.

On one level, this society and its hundreds of branches sought to reclaim "fallen women" and to prevent further immorality by teaching mothers how to train children to resist temptation.[19] In itself, praying in front of brothels, visiting prostitutes, and asserting that "ignorance is not purity" were departures from more "ladylike" activity. On another level, however, moral reformers demanded a restructuring of moral standards, an end to the double standard of sexuality that excluded a "fallen woman" from respectable society while it condoned the behavior of the "seducer." They sought to abolish this double standard not by having women act like men, but by demanding of men the same standards of virtue and passionlessness that society expected of women.[20]

If the society had restricted its activity to the salvation of prostitutes, it would have had little impact at Oberlin. Instead, it was the broadened attack on male behavior to which the Society found so many ready adherents in the rural community; virtually all female students joined. Alice Cowles became a vice-president of the national society, and Lydia Andrews Finney, Charles's wife, its first directress. By 1837, the Oberlin FMRS was the *fourth largest of 268 active moral reform auxiliaries*.[21] Admitting that "the vicious did not seek a house here,"[22] Oberlin members responded in a typical Oberlin manner; they took the critique of "male lust" to its logical conclusion and demanded complete purity of spirit. With few actual seducers to exclude from their company, Oberlin women vowed to shun not only those men who dared make illicit remarks or advances, but men who spoke disrespectfully of marriage or otherwise betrayed the rather exorbitant expectations of the women in their midst.[23]

Women were not alone in their commitment to moral reform. Men at Oberlin, in apparently sincere efforts to achieve this standard of purity, formed a male moral reform society, explicitly in support of the women's efforts.[24] It was the first male society to become an auxiliary to the national female organization, in itself (and even today) a remarkable act. The men shared the women's goals, reminding every young man not to feel complacent "till in his own experience he has realized all that the *spirit* of the Moral Reform Constitution requires—till every thought, and feeling, and impulse has been chastened into perfect obedience to the moral law."[25] The men joined the women in insisting that guilty females were less to blame than the sinful of their own sex. In 1835, however, after complimenting Oberlin men for establishing their auxiliary, the *Advocate of Moral Reform* chided Oberlin men for not stressing their sex's far greater blame for licentious behavior.[26] Men's vigilance in abolishing the double standard of sexual morality was closely watched by the women in the cause.

In general, Oberlin men tried to conform to a religious standard of behavior that was supposedly exemplified by the women in their midst. In 1839 several male students flogged a young man who had written impolite letters to a woman; when the faculty considered reprimanding the students, the young men gained the respect and ardent defense of the female students. Men struggled against accepting "worldly" standards for their behavior: "God grant me grace to avoid obstinacy and self confidence," prayed the young James Fairchild. "As a class," admitted an article in the *Oberlin Evangelist*, "young men are far enough from possessing virtuous hearts. . . ."[27] Its author encouraged men to follow their sisters diligently into moral reform activity that would lead, apparently, to their banishing even thoughts that were sinful. The moral reform movement established a single standard for behavior for women and men. Equally important, it provided a mechanism by which men could demonstrate their commitment to virtue. Only by adhering to this so-called female standard could Oberlin hope to achieve the level of harmony and virtue it desired.

Even the most strident efforts to infuse the experiment with Christian virtue could not, of course, prevent conflict within the Oberlin community; not surprisingly, these conflicts often focused on the boundaries of acceptable female behavior. Much has been made, and rightfully, of the demands of feminists Lucy Stone and Antoinette Brown for identical access to the prerogatives of men, in particular the right to read commencement addresses to mixed audiences and to receive theological diplomas.[28] Less easily explained, from our perspective, is an 1839 confrontation between Professors Asa Mahan and James Thome, and a group of female students. Apparently, Mahan had proposed that a large class of women from the Ladies' Department be distributed among the male college classes, where they would exert a good influence on the men (and, incidentally, read their compositions aloud in a mixed setting). Twenty-three young women petitioned the faculty against this change; in spite of Mahan's private pressure on them, they stood firm, declaring that modesty prevented them from reading in the college classes. Professor Thome remarked in a faculty meeting that "it was a false modesty, or delicacy, and . . . they would soon get used to it."[29] Alice Cowles prevailed in defense of the young women, however, and only those women who chose to take the college classes (as many did) would read before men.

This is more than a case of "false modesty," as Professor Thome would have it, or "false consciousness," as would some historians. Clearly, some women maintained a commitment to different behavior for women and men in a coeducational setting. What is striking about this incident is that the women's action was largely symbolic; isolation of women from men was never implemented at Oberlin, and these same women must have interacted with their fellow students in numerous other settings. Moreover, they would not have been the first women to recite in college classes. Yet symbolic behavior was, after all, of central importance to the model community. If women were to set the standard for purity in a mixed setting, they would have to preserve their distinctiveness in some particulars. Being "modest," satisfied with "private" proofs of achievement, submitting one's ego to close and painful scrutiny—these signified the female virtues that Oberlin wished to inspire. Oberlin women approached the task of being role models for men with the fervor with which they assumed all aspects of their Christian duty. In pressing publicly their claim to distinct female behavior, these twenty-three young women acted within an already-established Oberlin tradition: they exacted of themselves an ever higher standard of "female" virtue. They should not be dismissed as simply "conservative." Their action reflected a shared belief in the necessity for heightening female qualities, including delicacy, especially in the face of charges that delicacy was precisely what was lacking in the model Christian community.

For the outside world did not react to Oberlin as intended. However conservative the college's vision of a future society may seem, Oberlin's neighbors judged its abolitionism, religious fervor, and missionary intentions as threatening to traditional lifestyles and values. Hannah Warner, an Oberlin student, taught school in Avon, Ohio, during vacations. She taught of the love of God, she explained, but not of "Oberlinisms," as she found people bitterly opposed. She felt that to speak of "smaller things," such as the need to deny the "superfluities of life," would remind her students and their parents of Oberlin, and antagonize them.[30] Delazon Smith, a student who had been expelled and excommunicated for his aggressive attacks on the Christian religion, published an "unmasking" of Oberlin in 1837; he described the "lewdness and extreme depravity" which allegedly resulted from allowing women and men of both races to comingle.[31] The neighboring communities did not respond tolerantly to such descriptions. Rumors circulated that some critics intended to burn the college buildings; other Ohioans merely heckled speakers from the college.[32] Both church and state tried to limit Oberlin's influence. The Presbytery denied ordination to James Fairchild and his brother Edward because they refused to regard "the influence of Oberlin as pernicious."[33] Ohio legislators, who tried and failed six times to revoke the College's charter, agreed that Oberlin was "dangerous to liberty, law and morality," largely because of its antislavery activity.[34] Legislator Josiah Harris wrote his wife of the tremendous opposition to the school; there were "a thousand unfavorable rumors in relation to the amalgamation, fanaticism, harboring fugitive slaves, etc., all founded upon rumor. . . ."[35] Isolated from the surrounding community, Oberlin in its early years focused intensely on the internal state of religion, on training abolitionists and missionaries, and on creating a model which only awaited the world's welcome. In the meantime, Oberlin was in a world of its own.

The experiment, of course, failed. Oberlin never recreated the world in its own image, nor could it maintain for very long the intense commitment to perfection that its early faculty and students had demanded of themselves. By 1850, for a variety of reasons, the period of what Fletcher called "peculiar Oberlin" had ended.[36] In part, this can be attributed to increasing heterogeneity among students, decreasing abhorrence of such "Oberlinisms" as abolition and coeducation, and the lessening influence of men like Asa Mahan. In addition, the late 1840s saw a shift among reformers toward electoral politics and away from the rhetoric, indeed, the fervor, of the evangelical years. This transition away from moral suasion meant a shift away from "female values" and toward a more secular political style. In many cases, this new emphasis isolated women from the center of reform activity and ideology; it seems to me no coincidence that women reformers added suffrage to their demands in 1848. The reform fervor of the next generation of Oberlin students was directed less toward individual perfection than toward legislative change. It should not be surprising that this trend coincided with a general denigration of so-called female virtues among reformers.[37] It was only in the first decade or so of its existence that Oberlin students tried to build a community in which all its members would adopt and make universal those qualities that they considered not only Christian, but feminine.

I am by no means suggesting that unequal power relations between women and men were absent from early Oberlin or that they would have been obliterated by the model Oberlin sought to establish. What I am suggesting, however, is that it is inadequate to characterize that experiment as conservative simply because of the persistence of ideologically defined gender spheres. The founders and students at Oberlin sought to create a harmonious community which not only assumed traditional gender roles, but which demanded that both women and men conform to the standards supposedly established in the domestic sphere—that is, characteristics largely attributed to women. In condemning Oberlin for "conservative" values, for its putatively traditional views of gender roles, historians have denigrated the very values that Oberlin sought to emphasize. Oberlin urged all people to reject "male values" in the interest of a self-sacrificing, community-oriented nation.

Herein lie the radical implications of Oberlin's vision. Ultimately, if female characteristics were not intrinsic to women, but learned—that is, if men could adopt them—the very notion of "gender spheres" would be subject to attack. The possibility that men could become "like" women had the potential of undermining an elaborate system of rationalizing sexual inequality, a threat that has apparently been even more difficult to accept than the idea of women being able to achieve on the level of men. Oberlin's founders, of course, did not recognize this contradiction in their philosophy, although they did recognize the challenge to "worldly," or "male," privileges that it implied. Women and men at early Oberlin called for, and tried to create, a world in which traditional Christian virtues, considered inherent in women, defined the standard for all people's behavior. Their analysis, if not their fervor, appealed to many nineteenth-century women, as well as to many in the 1980s, who seek a "higher" standard for female behavior in exchange for the "prerogatives" of women's traditional role and, significantly, for some control over *men's* behavior.[38] Early Oberlin bequeathed a disquieting vision to those later feminists who would seek to "raise" women to men's level without reordering the power relations inherent in the hierarchy itself. They left, to be glimpsed in their contradictions, the critique of the concept of inherent gender traits to a still later generation, possibly our own.

NOTES

For assistance in writing this essay I would like to thank Jeanne Boydston, William Cronon, and Joel Steiker. Carol Lasser was a tremendous help as the editor of this volume. I am also grateful to my friends at Oberlin, especially Geoffrey Blodgett, Marlene Merrill, and Dan Merrill for their continuing support and enthusiasm.

1. John N. Laurvik, "Articles on the American Girl," *American Educational Review* 33 (June 1912), quoted in Thomas Woody, *A History of Women's Education* (New York: Science Press, 1929), 2: 271.

2. See Frances Juliette Hosford, *Father Shipherd's Magna Charta: A Century of Coeducation in Oberlin College* (Boston: Marshall Jones, 1937); James H. Fairchild, *Oberlin: The Colony and the College* (Oberlin: By the author, 1883), pp. 174–75. Fairchild noted that plans for a wholly separate female department, as proposed in the first circular, were never implemented; women, he claimed, entered the project as they would a household, "because they belonged in the enterprise," not because of any "special theoretical views on the subject" (p. 175).

3. See especially Ronald Hogeland, " 'Co-education of the Sexes' at Oberlin College: A Study of Social Ideas in Mid-Nineteenth-Century America," *Journal of Social History* 6: 2 (Winter 1972–73): 160–76; Jill Conway, "Perspectives on the History of Women's Education in the United States," *History of Education Quarterly* 14: 1 (Spring 1974): 1–12. For an opposing view, see Lori D. Ginzberg, "Women in an Evangelical Community: Oberlin, 1835–50," *Ohio History* 89 (Winter 1980): 78–88.

4. "Prudential Report," *Oberlin Evangelist*, December 3, 1851. Oberlin's original purpose is best stated in its own "Covenant of the Oberlin Colony," a copy of which is in Box 11, Robert Fletcher Collection, Oberlin College Archives, Oberlin, Ohio (OCA).

5. On the revivals, see Paul E. Johnson, *A Shopkeeper's Millennium: Society and Revivals in Rochester, New York, 1815–1837* (New York: Hill and Wang, 1978); Whitney R. Cross, *The Burned-Over District: The Social and Intellectual History of Enthusiastic Religion in Western New York, 1800–1850* (Ithaca, N.Y.: Cornell University Press, 1950; repr. New York: Harper Torchbooks, 1965). On Oberlin's place in this upheaval and in the world of reform in general, see Robert Samuel Fletcher, *A History of Oberlin College: From Its Foundations through the Civil War*, 2 vols. (Oberlin, Ohio: Oberlin College, 1943).

6. Kathryn Kish Sklar, *Catharine Beecher: A Study in American Domesticity* (New York: W. W. Norton, 1976), especially chap. 11, pp. 151–67.

7. "Covenant of the Oberlin Colony."

8. Hogeland, "Coeducation of the Sexes," p. 164. See also Fletcher, *History of Oberlin College,* I: 381, for the reluctant admission of Professor John Morgan that women's influence "worked."

9. Charles Finney address, *Oberlin Evangelist*, September 10, 1851. Quoted in Hogeland, "Coeducation of the Sexes," p. 163.

10. Diaries and letters of Oberlin women located in the Oberlin College Archives expressed the (inevitable) sense of failure in living up to these extreme standards of purity. For a fascinating comparison of evangelical women's and men's religious experiences, and the difficulty of living up to the female ideal, see Barbara Epstein, *The Politics of Domesticity: Women, Evangelism and Temperance in Nineteenth-Century America* (Middletown, Conn.: Wesleyan University Press, 1981), pp. 45–66.

11. Minutes of the Meeting of the Board of Trustees, Oberlin College, March 9, 1836, OCA. See also *Religious Intelligence,* October 1, 1836: informed opinion, asserted the article, knew that the "grossness and vulgarity" of men's colleges were absent from Oberlin.

12. Fletcher, *History of Oberlin College,* II: 809.

13. Nancy Prudden to George Prudden, May 15, 1837, Box 11, Fletcher Collection, OCA; Ann Elisa Gillett to Charlotte Fenner, January 5, 1838, Box 7, Fletcher Collection, OCA.

14. Louis D. Hartson, "Marriage Records of Alumnae for the First Century of a Coeducational College," *Journal of Heredity* 31: 9 (September 1940): 403–06. It should not be surprising that Oberlin women married more frequently than did women at single-sex colleges; more significantly, they married Oberlin men—or like-minded ministers and teachers—with startling consistency. On Holley and Putnam, see John White Chadwick, ed., *A Life for Liberty: Anti-Slavery and Other Letters of Sallie Holley* (New York: G. P. Putnam's Sons, 1899).

15. Fletcher, *History of Oberlin College,* II: 644, 640.

16. A. L. Shumway and C. Dew. Brower, *Oberliniana* (Cleveland: Home Publishing, [1883?]), p. 88.

17. Quoted in Alice Stone Blackwell, *Lucy Stone: Pioneer of Woman's Rights* (Boston: Little, Brown, 1930), p. 50. Stone may have misremembered one particular; given the Grahamite principles of many Oberlinians, it is unlikely that they drank coffee during her college years.

18. Sklar, *Catharine Beecher,* p. 135.

19. On the moral reform movement, see Carroll Smith-Rosenberg, "Beauty, the Beast and the Militant Woman: A Case Study of Sex Roles and Social Stress in Jacksonian America," *American Quarterly* 23 (October 1971): 562–84; Barbara J. Berg, *The Remembered Gate: Origins of American Feminism* (New York: Oxford University Press, 1978).

20. Nancy F. Cott, "Passionlessness: An Interpretation of Victorian Sexual Ideology, 1790–1850," *Signs* 4 (Winter 1978): 219–36.

21. Fletcher, *History of Oberlin College,* I: 301. It was founded with 380 women as members. Oberlin Female Moral Reform Society Annual Report (1840), OFMRS Records, OCA. The records and minutes of the OFMRS are fairly complete and are all in the Oberlin College Archives.

22. OFMRS Annual Report (1840), OCA.

23. See Fletcher, *History of Oberlin College,* I: 300–315, for a discussion of the Oberlin FMRS.

24. Lawrence J. Friedman, in *Gregarious Saints: Self and Community in American Abolitionism, 1830–1870* (New York: Cambridge University Press, 1982), discusses men's emulation of female models of behavior among ultraist abolitionists. Some, he writes, "seemed desirous of . . . imbibing a profound female moral and emotional strength that was missing in themselves" (p. 156).

25. *Oberlin Evangelist,* October 9, 1839. See also Fletcher, *History of Oberlin College,* I: 299–300.

26. *Advocate of Moral Reform* 8 (1835): 57.

27. The flogging incident is described in Fletcher, *History of Oberlin College,* I: 444–46; Fairchild to Mary Kellogg, September 21, 1851, in "Where Liberty Dwells, Letters 1838–41," typescript in Oberlin College Special Collections; *Oberlin Evangelist,* August 14, 1839.

28. On the experience of these activists at Oberlin see especially Carol Lasser and Marlene Merrill, eds., *Soul Mates: The Oberlin Correspondence of Lucy Stone and Antoinette Brown, 1846–1850* (Oberlin, Ohio: Oberlin College, 1983); Elizabeth Cazden, *Antoinette Brown Blackwell: A Biography* (Old Westbury, N.Y.: Feminist Press, 1983). I have no intention of lessening the important and far-seeing nature of the demands of these and other feminists at Oberlin and elsewhere. Rather, I wish to highlight the frequently overlooked aspect of the Oberlin experience: the creation of a female standard of behavior and morality that men were expected to uphold.

29. John P. Cowles to the *Ohio Observer,* November 13 and 20, 1839. See also, Fletcher, *History of Oberlin College,* I: 294.

30. Hannah Warner to her parents, December 24, 1841, January 28, 1842, Box 16, Fletcher Collection, OCA.

31. Delazon Smith, *A History of Oberlin, or New Lights of the West* (Cleveland: S. Underhill and Son, 1837). On Smith himself, see Fletcher, *History of Oberlin College,* I: 436–41.

32. Fairchild, *Oberlin: Colony and College,* p. 116.

33. Fairchild to Kellogg, September 21, 1840, in "Where Liberty Dwells." See Fletcher, *History of Oberlin College,* I: 226–27.

34. Clayton S. Ellsworth, "Ohio's Legislative Attack upon Abolitionist Schools," *Mississippi Valley Historical Review* 21 (December 1934): 379–86.

35. Fairchild, *Oberlin: Colony and College,* p. 368.

36. Fletcher, *History of Oberlin College,* II: 886.

37. See George M. Frederickson, *The Inner Civil War: Northern Intellectuals and the Crisis of the Union* (New York: Harper and Row, 1965). Frederickson describes a similar phenomenon occurring during—and because of—the Civil

War. See also Lori D. Ginzberg, "Women and the Work of Benevolence: Morality and Politics in the Northeastern United States, 1820–1885," Ph.D. diss., Yale University, 1985.

38. See Barbara Ehrenreich, *The Hearts of Men: American Dreams and the Flight from Commitment* (New York: Anchor Books, 1983), especially chap. 10, "The Backlash," for a perceptive analysis of right-wing women's efforts to "tame" men. See also Andrea Dworkin, *Right Wing Women* (New York: G. P. Putnam's Sons, 1981). Both authors describe a twentieth-century version of women's efforts to limit male "lust" in order to protect themselves—and, supposedly, all women—from men themselves.

The Oberlin Model and Its Impact on Other Colleges

BARBARA MILLER SOLOMON

In 1833, evangelical fervor quite unexpectedly spawned a collegiate model for the joint education of the sexes in the wilderness of Ohio; at Oberlin men and women (and shortly, white and black) were educated together to carry out God's cause on earth. To outsiders in 1833 the idea was bizarre, an aberration. Fifty years later, however, what Charles Finney called "God's College"[1] was well known as the model for many other institutions with similar strong religious commitments. Moreover, the Oberlin way of educating men and women provided a source of inspiration and support for educators introducing or struggling with coeducation at a variety of secular institutions. Why and how had Oberlin's experiment with joint education become a success story over the years? Both the Oberlin development of coeducation and the responses to it had positive and negative elements that shaped the character of this experiment, defined its limits, and influenced the next stage of coeducation. The Oberlin model represented the beginning of a long, complex process that is still evolving.

Admitting women represented a bigger step than the founders fully understood; the evangelical leaders intended no more than to prepare men and women better for their appointed duties in life. But without precedents for joint collegiate instruction, the faculty and administrators developed patterns that made plain the inherent paradoxes of Oberlin's nineteenth-century coeducation: women were taken seriously, not regarded as "toys or playthings," but nevertheless men were, and were to remain, the "leading sex."[2] As President Fairchild recalled in 1867,

Oberlin education was to "fit men and women for any position or work
to which they might properly be called."[3] The adverb "properly" was
significant in retaining traditional roles for men and women.

There was no consensus about the extent to which women should
study in the liberal arts curriculum. The founders had a vision of educated men who would become ministers and of educated women who
would become ministers' wives. To this end, all students, irrespective of
sex, took a portion of the set curriculum together: English, history, moral
philosophy, and some sciences and mathematics. But questions of curricular propriety soon arose: Did women need to study the ancient
languages? Although Oberlin professors disagreed about how much and
which classical literature (which had, after all, been written by "hea-
thens") was beneficial for anyone, they nonetheless recognized the need
for some such studies by future ministers. In the end, the modified Ladies'
Course excluded Latin, Greek, and Hebrew.

Initially, the Administration responded with resistance to the request
of a few women who had already studied Greek and Latin that they be
allowed to take the regular degree like the men. The request was, however, granted; three women earned the A.B. in 1841.[4] Thereafter women
were not excluded from the more demanding program, but neither were
they obliged to choose it. For the majority of female students, the Ladies'
Course apparently sufficed. The Ladies' Course, permanently renamed
the Literary Course in 1875, had even attracted some men.[5]

Even though most women received the certificate of the modified
program, Oberlin educators often noted that in any branch of study "the
best scholar" was just as likely to be a young woman as a young man."[6]
President James Fairchild thus concluded that there was no study "that
would not be helpful in the discipline and furniture of an educated
lady."[7] And yet, women were to use collegiate education within their
own sphere, not in the public one occupied by men.

Very few females challenged Oberlin in this period to provide full
equality in higher education through access to every type of training and
through public certification of what they accomplished. One who did
was Antoinette Brown, who came already determined to be a minister.
Her idol, Charles Finney (the minister who had converted her in childhood), could not justify to himself excluding this devout, serious, able
young woman from his classes in the graduate theological course, but
neither he nor anyone else at Oberlin was willing to give her the diploma,

quite apart from ordaining her as a minister. Nor did Antoinette Brown press the institution hard on these critical matters. However, her peers in the program ignored precedent and welcomed her into their exclusively male theological literary society.[8]

Even women who received the A.B. degree could not read essays at commencement, the occasion where young men showed their oratorical abilities in the company of the trustees, parents, and supporters of the college. It is well known that Lucy Stone refused to follow the pattern of reading her essay the night before at the women's separate pre-commencement gathering. Not until 1858 was an Oberlin woman allowed to read her own part at the regular commencement; not until 1874 did one cast aside her written part and orate like an Oberlin man.[9]

The ban on female public speaking became the symbol of the division of the sexes to be upheld regardless of an individual's education. Many faculty and students became more rigid in their allegiance to the tradition in order to dissociate Oberlin from the increasingly visible female public lecturers in the antislavery and woman's rights causes. Although Oberlin had its rebels and nonconformists, tensions over reading English compositions in a new joint rhetoric class exploded when many women, reluctant to read before men, insisted on separate classes for this exercise and thus brought to an end a small coeducational experiment.[10]

Undoubtedly many students of both sexes felt more comfortable abiding by separate activities, and the college reinforced this attitude in a variety of ways. As in a family, so at Oberlin male professors supervised the behavior of the male students while the Ladies' Department Board had charge of women. The "lady principals," themselves products of the New England female academies of Zilpah Grant and Mary Lyon (or of early Oberlin), exerted a powerful influence for the maintenance of evangelical moral standards for the young women. Social rules clearly demarcated the access of students to the opposite sex. The library was used by men at one time and by women at another. The classrooms and the dining table, as well as choir rehearsals, offered the most opportunities for men and women to communicate, although under supervision. Even areas and times for walking were prescribed, and of course there was no dancing.[11]

For the most part, students associated with members of their own sex in any number of extracurricular activities. They had literary and moral reform societies; the women had maternal associations as well. In their separate forums outside the classroom, men and women might more freely express themselves. Among peers of the same sex one could consider controversial questions about marriage and single life or about woman suffrage. Of course, no organization could exist without approval from the authorities. The Ladies' Department closely regulated the women's clubs. Lucy Stone's request for a debating society was denied, as was another request from women to have a literary magazine.[12]

With its emphasis on propriety, Oberlin's mode of coeducation gave it an appearance of safety which may help explain the swiftness with which the joint education of the sexes spread. Other colleges in the Midwest soon followed Oberlin's initiative in educating men and women together. But equally important in this development was the economic factor. Similar rural communities could not afford any more than Oberlin to provide separate collegiate institutions. Oberlin's coeducation model spread in the 1840s, 1850s, and the early 1860s to several religious colleges, from the Midwest to the East. These included, among others, Olivet (Michigan), Ripon (Wisconsin), Grinnell (Iowa), Knox (Illinois), Northfield (Minnesota), and Antioch and Wilberforce, a black college (Ohio). Bates in Maine, Swarthmore in Pennsylvania, and Syracuse in New York also followed the Oberlin pattern. Although of different denominations—Congregationalist, Methodist, Unitarian, or Quaker— all shared the same Christian values about the relationships of men and women. At Swarthmore the evangelical and feminist supporters of coeducation converged; the collegiate pattern, however, resembled that of Oberlin, where men and women gathered at meals for civilized discourse.[13]

After the Civil War, white and black graduates of Oberlin took the lead in sustaining schools for freed men and women. Berea, Howard, Fisk, and Talladega, for example, all embraced the same evangelical ideal and the same coeducational pattern, even though men at first predominated in the classes.[14] Oberlin black women like Mary Jane Patterson, Fanny Jackson Coppin, and Anna Julia Cooper transmitted this heritage to the black high-school students they prepared for college attendance.[15]

Adapting the Oberlin model, other denominational colleges developed their own particular variations on coeducation. Most had a ladies' course and separate extracurricular societies. Not all had a residential hall for women. And most retained fairly conservative religious views of the meaning of women's higher education. President Jonathan Blanchard, describing the Knox College experience in the *Independent* in 1870, stressed that the relationship between men and women was not changed by college education. He remarked, "Adam and Eve got their education together in Eden; and . . . their sons and daughters should do so in the schools, though the sons may name the cattle, and the daughters dress the flowers."[16]

Oberlin's evangelical experiment also became the focus of attention for secular educators facing the challenges of coeducation for public and private institutions in the 1870s. The Civil War had brought more women into the sphere of higher education to fill places vacated by men, and implementation of the Morrill Act of 1862, which led to the establishment of public land-grant institutions, intensified the struggle over women's admission. Although few in numbers, by 1870 determined females all over the country clamored for admission to a variety of public and private institutions. Liberal educators under pressure sought evidence to justify to conservative critics the admission of women. Oberlin became a highly valued source of information on how coeducation worked in practice. Educators counted on Oberlin for answers to a whole series of questions about joint instruction: the educability of women; the behavioral effects on men and women of studying together; what was good for each sex; and what was good for the institution.

The key questions were those of social propriety: How did students of both sexes behave in the joint educational setting? On this point, Oberlin's experience gave reassurance. One discerning Oberlin professor told English visitors in 1871 that "the system answers very well with us. . . . We find that the presence of the girls has a good effect upon the men and that of the men upon the girls. We think that the girls if kept away from young men will be dreaming about them, and it is better that they should see them. Nothing acts as a better antidote for romance than young men and women doing geometry together at eight o'clock every morning."[17]

Liberal educators also confronted old prejudices against educating women which took new forms when so-called scientific studies claimed that advanced education would endanger women's health. Dr. Edward H. Clarke's "scientific" study *Sex in Education*, published in 1873, did not deny that women were educable, but insisted they could not study and "retain uninjured health and a future secure from neuralgia, uterine disease, hysteria, and other derangements of the nervous system."[18] Clarke shifted the question from that of woman's rights to the welfare of society. He believed that if women were to fulfill their biological functions as childbearers, then their collegiate education must be halted. Thus women's social roles and educational aspirations seemed in unalterable opposition.

Educators in need of refuting Clarke turned repeatedly to Oberlin's experience. In 1867 President Fairchild had already reported to a group of midwestern college presidents that at his school "a breaking down in health" occurred no more among the young women than among the young men.[19] Two educators especially made good use of Fairchild's evidence: in 1872 President Andrew Dickson White of Cornell, under pressure to admit women, called on Fairchild to bolster his positive evaluation of coeducation, and a decade later, W. Le Conte Stevens, professor at Packard Institute in Brooklyn, N.Y., looked to Oberlin when conducting his investigation on behalf of women's admission to Columbia. The reports of White and Stevens relied largely on Oberlin's record to sever the connection Dr. Clarke had made between advanced female education and the poor health of many American women. Both men, however, expressed concern with protecting women's mental and physical well-being; thus they noted that the absence of prizes and public grades at Oberlin eased the strain of study on conscientious students, likely to be female.[20] Whether or not it was following Oberlin's example, it is interesting that coeducational Stanford, progressive at its opening in the 1880s, also gave no grades; similarly, for a longer time such women's colleges as Wellesley, Smith, Mount Holyoke, and Vassar did not inform students of their grades. Increasingly after 1900, however, marking was instituted at most colleges. We may speculate that grades served as an index of the increasing acceptance of competition on every campus, coeducational and single-sex.

If competition in education gradually became acceptable, many still feared that its adverse effects might spill into the private sphere. It was not clear that the newly acquired sense of competitiveness could be reconciled with the continuing expectation that women be dutiful wives. During Oberlin's first fifty years, the high marital rates of alumnae reassured a public fearful of the impact of education on fertility. Although these rates were interpreted positively, they were not accurate indicators of future trends. In the changing academic milieus of the early twentieth century, women's patterns of marriage and childbearing would remain a critical issue. Of the women enrolled in Oberlin in 1840, all but one reported themselves married or widowed in an 1860 survey. In 1883 it was noted that the work of four-fifths of the women "centres on the home life," while one-fifth of the women "are filling responsible positions in America and abroad, doing a work which the world needs."[21]

Oberlin had provided the first proofs that coeducation would not endanger the development of men, women, or American society. Yet the uses made of the Oberlin evidence were double edged; it could be cited to advance education for both sexes, but it could also be used to keep women back. By 1883, for example, 702 Oberlin women had taken the Literary Course while only 133 had completed the full course, from which the vast majority of men had been graduated. Because most women chose the less demanding program, their choices could fortify the argument in the scientific jargon of the day that "the physical organization of the female has a reflex influence on the intellectual manifestations of the sex."[22]

Such curricular distinctions reinforced traditional views of women's intellectual inferiority. Educators White and Stevens, among others, cited the success of separate male and female courses of study to support the introduction of academic electives in the university curriculum. Although there were compelling rationales to promote electives, the assumption that electives would permit women to take not only different but easier courses than men had negative implications for the next stage of coeducation at institutions that were competing for academic excellence. At Oberlin itself, the fight for electives in the 1890s represented demands for an expansive and more rigorous education, but there and elsewhere traditional gender stereotypes could cloud academic innovation. The so-called feminization of certain subjects and fields would later create new problems.[23]

The paradoxes of coeducation multiplied over time; expansion in numbers of male and female students, changes in social mores, increasing variety in the student body, as well as academic curricular changes: these would influence the development of coeducation in the twentieth century. Many unforeseeable problems in coeducation lay ahead, and some have yet to be resolved.

The founding of Oberlin fulfilled a religious ideal in new ways and thus brought women part of the way into the male world of academia. Even the once-rebellious students as alumnae in later life paid tribute to Oberlin for its pioneering effort, which made their collegiate education a reality. Although the first Oberlin women did not have equality in the modern sense, they knew that, despite restrictions, they were respected. As it has outgrown the original evangelical model it created in 1833,

Oberlin still retains one distinct advantage: it has always taken women seriously.

NOTES

I would like to express appreciation to Carol Lasser for her sensitive prodding as editor; my thanks to Sandy Peacock for helpful suggestions and for work on sources at Oberin College. In addition it should be noted that some of the material in this essay appears in my book, *In the Company of Educated Women: A History of Women and Higher Education in America* (New Haven, Conn.: Yale University Press, 1985).

1. Robert S. Fletcher, *A History of Oberlin College: From Its Foundation through the Civil War*, 2 vols. (Oberlin, Ohio: Oberlin College, 1943), I: 208.

2. "The idea that the young lady is a toy or a plaything is very thoroughly exploded by the practical working of intellectual competition on the college race ground." Quoted from the *Oberlin Evangelist*, June 7, 1854, in Robert Fletcher, *A History of Oberlin College*, 1: 379.

3. James H. Fairchild's 1867 address is quoted in James Orton, ed., *The Liberal Education of Women: The Demand and the Method, Current Thoughts in America and England* (New York: A. S. Barnes, 1873), p. 247.

4. Robert Fletcher, *A History of Oberlin College*, I: 380

5. James H. Fairchild, *Oberlin: The Colony and the College, 1833–1883* (Oberlin, Ohio: E. J. Goodrich, 1883), p. 181.

6. Ibid., p. 184.

7. James H. Fairchild, quoted in James Orton, ed., *The Liberal Education of Women*, p. 247.

8. Yet, in 1853, because of her Oberlin training but without the institution's approval, Antoinette Brown was ordained as a Congregationalist minister to a small congregation in South Butler, New York. For further information, see Barbara Miller Solomon, "Antoinette Brown Blackwell," in Edward T. James et al., eds., *Notable American Women* (Cambridge, Mass.: Harvard University Press, 1971). See also Elizabeth Cazden, *Antoinette Brown Blackwell: A Biography* (Old Westbury, N.Y.: Feminist Press, 1983).

9. Robert Fletcher, *A History of Oberlin College*, I: 295, documents that Mary Raley was the first female graduate to read her own composition at commencement in 1858; Fairchild, *Oberlin*, p. 181, refers to young women regularly reading their essays from 1859.

10. Robert Fletcher, *A History of Oberlin College*, I: 291–94. We are all indebted to Lori Ginzberg for her original interpretation of early Oberlin and women's place in it. However, I am less certain than she about how to assess the

motives of the young women who insisted on separate composition classes. Ginzberg points out that they resisted pressure from President Mahan. But were they not also under considerable pressure from the lady principal, Alice Cowles? Also, might not some who took the high moral ground have preferred separate classes for personal reasons?

11. Robert Fletcher, *A History of Oberlin College,* II: 665–87.

12. Ibid., I: 290–340, 373–85.

13. On Oberlin's influence on other colleges, see ibid., II: 904. See also Edward H. Magill, *An Address upon the Co-Education of the Sexes* (Philadelphia: Charles A. Dixon, 1873).

14. Fletcher, *A History of Oberlin College,* II: 909ff.

15. Ibid., II: 534ff. See also Leona Gabel, "Anna Julia Cooper," in Barbara Sicherman and Carol Hurd Green, eds., *Notable American Women: The Modern Period* (Cambridge, Mass.: Harvard University Press, 1980).

16. President Blanchard, "The Experience at Knox College," in *The Independent,* is quoted in Orton, *The Liberal Education of Women,* pp. 260–65.

17. For example, The Honorable Dudley Campbell, visiting in 1871, first published an essay, "Mixed Education for Boys and Girls in England and America," in *The Contemporary Review* in 1872. Quoted in Fletcher, *A History of Oberlin College,* II: 905.

18. Edward H. Clarke, *Sex in Education* (Boston: J. R. Osgood, 1873).

19. President Fairchild is quoted in Orton, *The Liberal Education of Women,* p. 246.

20. Andrew D. White, *Report Submitted to the Trustees of Cornell University on Behalf of a Majority of the Committee on Mr. Sage's Proposal to Endow a College for Women* (Ithaca, N.Y.: Cornell, 1872). A relevant portion was reprinted as "Effects of Co-Education on Young Women" in James Orton, ed., *The Liberal Education of Women,* pp. 217–23. W. Le Conte Stevens, *The Admission of Women to Universities, Testimony Gathered in Connection with an Essay, in the North American Review for January, 1883, on "University Education for Women"* (New York, 1883). W. Le Conte Stevens, "University Education for Women," *North American Review* 136 (January, 1883): 24–39, especially 37. Information about the grading problem appears in college records.

21. Fairchild, *Oberlin,* p. 185.

22. Figures are found in ibid., pp. 184–85. John Le Conte, quoted in W. Le Conte Stevens, *The Admission of Women to Universities,* p. 9.

23. See John Barnard, *From Evangelicalism to Progressivism at Oberlin College, 1866–1917* (Columbus: Ohio State University Press, 1969). See also Sydney D. Strong and Merritt Starr, *Proportions of Men and Women Enrolled as Students at Oberlin College: A Report to the Trustees* (1905). In a crisis when the number of women exceeded that of men, the recommendations in this report

opposed arbitrary limitations but urged "affirmative measures to attract the attendance of men," p. 21; I thank Marlene Merrill for alerting me to this report.

In addition to the works cited above, I benefited from reading Lori Ginzberg, "Women in an Evangelical Community: Oberlin 1835–1850" in *Ohio History*, 89 (1980); and Sally Schwager, "Arguing for the Higher Education of Women: Early Experiences with Coeducation," Qualifying Paper, Harvard School of Education, June 1978.

Coeducation or Women's Education? A Comparison of Alumnae from Two Colleges: 1934–79

JANET ZOLLINGER GIELE

What type of educational environment is better for a young woman—a setting where she learns alongside young men, or one from which males are excluded? My own experience as a student in a coeducational college and university, then as a teacher in an all-women's school, and currently in a coeducational university, has been somewhat contradictory. It led to my current research on the women graduates of a Seven Sisters college, and Oberlin as a representative coeducational college in the Midwest. The question of what educational environment is "better" for a women has no simple answer. Nor is it clear how much credit for women's achievements should be accorded colleges compared with parents or luck.

My initial research questions came out of personal encounters with coeducation and single-sex education, and they were complicated by being at the same time immensely positive yet surprising in what it meant to be a woman student. Let me explain.

My own college experience had something in common with those of the women graduates of some of the first coeducational institutions, such as the University of Michigan or Oberlin. I had grown up in northeastern Ohio and in the mid-1950s had attended a coeducational Quaker college in Indiana. Over the course of my four college years I experienced tremendous support and friendship from my professors, and I achieved an outstanding academic record. Just before graduation, however, on the eve of accepting a coveted fellowship and entering graduate school, one of my professors, a famous Quaker, asked me kindly whether I really wanted to go to graduate school. He gently reminded me that women usually get married and have children. His question utterly startled me; it was so out of keeping with all that I had been led to expect. Yet it revealed to me a well-meaning sex bias that I have only lately come to recognize as latent in many educational settings that pride themselves on equal treatment of women.

At Harvard I also experienced exciting opportunities but at the same time a subtle devaluation of women's pursuits. In 1959, after several years of graduate study, I chose a dissertation topic on the woman suffrage and temperance movements. The chairman of the Committee on Higher Degrees, a humane and prominent professor, asked me another surprising question: "Are you sure you want to do a dissertation on women? All the women do dissertations on women." He asked the committee secretary to pull out the list and showed it to me. Although I still did my thesis on women, these personal experiences later made me realize the perseverance and determination required of a woman to succeed in a coeducational environment, even when she is an outstanding student surrounded by well-meaning faculty.

Until my first full-time position as a college teacher, I never seriously considered the alternative of all-female education. All my educational experience had been in coeducational environments—public schools, college, and graduate school. After finishing graduate school, however, I taught for one year in a Catholic women's college, then joined the faculty of one of the Seven Sisters. This world also had its contradictions. My fellow professors in 1962 took no particular notice of the fact that all their students were young women. Such obliviousness to gender was in many ways liberating and nondiscriminatory, but in other respects it denied the reality of women's lives. Yet seeing other young women faculty having babies, doing research, and teaching full-time was probably one of the greatest gifts that women's education could have given to me. The successive women deans and presidents of the college were also living proof that women could succeed to the highest levels of academic and corporate responsibility.

These personal experiences raised for me some of the continuing questions that have shaped my recent research on women's lives. The central issue is how women construct a life course to combine work and family life, graduate education, geographic shifts, frustrations, and triumphs. What difference, if any, does coeducation make in a woman's life as compared with education in a women's college?

To answer these questions I embarked several years ago on a comparative study of women college graduates. In the summer of 1982, the Life Pattern Study Project (with funding from the Lilly Endowment) mailed questionnaires to selected classes who were graduated between 1934 and 1979. In all, we received 2,902 replies, a little more than 60 percent of the respondents who had been contacted.

The primary purpose of the project was to study alumnae as a source of data on how women's lives are changing. In an earlier analysis of the Wellesley College alumnae census of 1962 I had learned that the living alumnae were a window on social change because their collective lives spanned nearly a century. The Wellesley census elicited more than 16,000 replies, some from women who had graduated as early as 1900. By comparing the replies of different age groups, it was possible to observe change in women's life patterns since the turn of the century. The Life Patterns Study in 1982 held a similar promise for charting the lives of younger women. In addition, the movement for coeducation that took place in the early 1970s gave new interest to the issue of single-sex education compared with coeducation as a means for the advanced instruction of women.[1]

COLLEGE DIFFERENCES

Reading only the research literature of coeducation and single-sex education before 1982, what would one predict to be the differences between the women graduates of a coeducational college and those of a women's college? In the 1970s, the proponents of coeducation believed that women's presence in all-male colleges like Yale or Dartmouth would humanize the atmosphere for men. The advantage to women would be in having access to these high-status men's schools. Another reason for coeducation, more implicit than explicit, was that college life for women would somehow be more "realistic" than in an all-female college. Instead of working during the week and seeing men only on weekends, the integrated classroom would bring the sexes together in their work as well as in their leisure.[2]

The proponents of women's education, however, claimed that the women's colleges had produced a disproportionate number of outstanding graduates. In 1973 Elizabeth Tidball examined the backgrounds of women whose names appeared in *Who's Who of American Women*. The graduates of women's colleges were significantly overrepresented for their numbers in the population. In 1976 Tidball and Vera Kistiakowsky further reported in *Science* that colleges differed in their production of male and female Ph.D.s. By examining the Doctorate Records File, they traced collegiate origins of men and women who had received doctorates. The top colleges for men were somewhat different from those for women. Among the top twenty-four undergraduate colleges who had graduated the largest number of female Ph.D.s from 1920 to 1939 and 1950 to 1969, *one-third were women's colleges*—the Seven Sisters (Barnard, Bryn Mawr, Mount Holyoke, Radcliffe, Smith, Vassar, and Wellesley) plus Goucher.[3] Relatively speaking, only a tiny proportion of small coeducational schools ranked high in production of both male and female doctorates (Reed, Swarthmore, Antioch, Oberlin, Carleton, and Pomona). A more common pattern was for small coeducational colleges to produce high numbers of male but not female Ph.D.s.

Extrapolating from these findings, one might expect that the women graduates of Oberlin would display life patterns somewhat similar to those of the graduates of the Seven Sisters college, or, if anything, that these coeducational graduates would be less oriented toward work or combining work and family. Among the Seven Sisters graduates there might be a larger proportion who had received graduate education, were employed, and had achieved greater prominence through their occupational attainments. Consistent with their greater educational and occupational achievement, we might further speculate that fewer of them would be married and, among the married, there would be fewer with children.

Such predictions were not supported when measured against our data. Consider the overall results from the Life Patterns Survey that was conducted in the summer of 1982 for the classes of 1934 through 1979 from Oberlin and the Seven Sisters college, shown in Table 1.

Table 1. Life patterns of women graduates of 1934–79 (in percent)

	Oberlin	Seven Sisters College
Ever married	77	83
Childbearing	59	70
Graduate education	60	52
Currently employed (1982)	68	62
	N = 977	N = 1,269

Although the percentage differences are not enormous, they are all in the opposite direction from what would have been predicted. Moreover, except in current employment, the patterns are remarkably consistent across the ten age groups from the classes of 1934 through 1979. For example, in every class group except 1974, more coeducational alumnae received some postgraduate education (see Table 2). Overall, the pattern goes against the hypotheses that could be derived from past studies.

What shall we make out of these findings? It should be noted that some scholars had already raised important questions about Tidball's findings that women's colleges produced more women with outstanding achievements. Mary J. Oates, an economist, and Susan Williamson, a mathematician, both at Regis College, a Catholic women's school in Massachusetts, in 1978 raised new methodological and interpretative issues in the discussion of the advantages of all-women's colleges.[4] Oates and Williamson analyzed the occupations and baccalaureate origins of women listed in the 1974–75 edition of *Who's Who in America*. They discovered that the rate of production of outstanding women graduates of the 1930s was very much higher for the Seven Sisters colleges (61 per 10,000 graduates) than for either the non-Seven Sisters or the coeducational schools (18 per 10,000 graduates). This finding suggested to them the importance of background factors such as socioeconomic status that were correlated both with attendance at a Seven Sisters college and with a chance of being listed in *Who's Who*. One of the major questions that Oates and Williamson thus left in the minds of their readers was whether it was women's education or family background that accounted for the high rate of achievement among 1930s graduates of Barnard, Bryn Mawr, Mount Holyoke, Radcliffe, Smith, Vassar, and Wellesley.

There was also a subsidiary question of how women's lack of access to the prestigious Ivy League schools may have shaped the results. If the Seven Sisters (the women's equivalent of the Ivy League) were more selective in their admissions than other women's colleges, were the achievements of their graduates the result of the women's education or the nature and abilities of the students who attended them?

The 1982 Life Patterns Study contains relevant information on several of these questions. Our survey permitted comparison of the family origins of students who attended the two colleges. Family background of the Seven Sisters' graduates does differ from that of the coeducational graduates, but not in ways that one might easily predict, such as *amount of parents' education,* or *level of professional attainment.* Instead, it is the

Table 2. Components of role choice among coeducational and women's college alumnae, classes of 1934–79 (in percent)

Class Group[a]	Marriage[b]		Motherhood		Graduate Education		Employed in 1982	
	Coed	Women's	Coed	Women's	Coed	Women's	Coed	Women's
1934	81	94	63	86	52	38	22	20
1939	93	94	85	88	43	39	31	32
1944	92	96	87	92	46	35	57	42
1949	91	95	82	91	53	52	73	60
1954	94	97	91	92	61	44	67	68
1959	94	94	81	90	66	63	87	81
1964	88	88	73	81	82	62	79	72
1969	86	83	53	59	82	74	81	80
1974	62	67	29	24	71	74	76	78
1979	25	27	2	5	34	30	68	71
No. of responses	755	1,056	581	893	582	656	663	783
Total no. surveyed	977	1,269	977	1,269	977	1,269	977	1,269
% Responding[c]	77	83	59	70	60	52	68	62
Mean (%)[d]	81	84	66	71	59	51	64	60

[a]These figures probably do not represent the completed histories of women in the class groups of 1974–79.
[b]Ever married.
[c]Number divided by total. This percentage does not take into account the differences in the proportion of total responses contributed by each class group.
[d]The percentage for each college was derived by averaging the percentages of the ten class groups. This figure makes an adjustment for the fact that the age distribution of respondents is different for each college.

types of parents' occupations that differ. Twice as many fathers of the Seven Sisters' graduates were M.D.s (10 percent vs. 5 percent), and twice as many were owners and managers (32 percent vs. 16 percent). But three times as many of the Oberlin graduates' fathers were college teachers (9 percent vs. 3 percent), and nearly twice as many of the Oberlin fathers (17 percent vs. 10 percent) were physical scientists or engineers. More of the Oberlin fathers had a graduate or professional degree (52 percent) than the Seven Sisters' fathers (42 percent).

Perhaps even more striking are the background differences in the occupations and educations of the mothers. Many more of the women's college mothers (68 percent vs. 52 percent) were homemakers. Almost twice as many of the Oberlin mothers had graduate or professional degrees (22 percent vs. 13 percent). These mothers were more likely to project a model of combining work and family life than the Seven Sisters' mothers. The Oberlin mothers numbered more elementary and secondary school teachers (13 percent vs. 7 percent); more clerical and secretarial workers (6 percent vs. 4 percent); and more social workers (3 percent vs. 1 percent). On the surface at least, it seems plausible that the mother as role model was at least as strong a factor in shaping the graduates' life patterns as type of college education.

Possibly these background differences influenced a girl's selection of the type of college that she would attend. Whether by parental encouragement, student's own choice, or some other mechanism, the young women who attended each college were rather different in their goals and values. Each respondent was asked her reasons for choosing her college, her interests and goals, and what she now values most from her college experience. Although many answers were similar in mentioning an interest in learning and getting a good education, the two colleges differed markedly in the value that their graduates attached to political awareness and social consciousness. Many more of the Oberlin graduates said political awareness was very important in what they got out of their college experience (34 percent vs. 13 percent). Likewise, more of them (52 percent vs. 24 percent) rated increased social consciousness high in what they most valued from their college education.

Because both of these colleges were academically selective and had long histories of social consciousness and social service, it seems likely that value differences among the two groups of alumnae were not acquired in college but instead were brought by the students. These values then influenced the young women's choices in college life and stayed with them after graduation to shape their adult life patterns. Preliminary support for this interpretation comes from data on adult lives of the two groups of alumnae. The marital timing patterns, educational and occupational histories, and adult values of the two groups all differ in subtle but powerful ways. It is difficult to imagine the contrasts as due merely to four years in a particular college setting.

The timing of marriage is noticeably different for graduates of the two colleges. On average coeducational alumnae married about a year later than the women's college graduates. This pattern is evident even when only the currently employed from the two colleges are compared (Table 3). Oberlin graduates also have fewer children than alumnae of similar age and employment status from the Seven Sisters college (see Table 4). Within a few years of graduation, women graduates of Oberlin exhibited the later marriage timing patterns and the tendency to have fewer children that are typical of women attached to the labor force. The women's college graduates were slightly more likely to be homemakers.

To what factors should we attribute these differences? Family role models? Personal values? College training? Whatever the process, the coeducated women constructed a somewhat different "role package" in adulthood. Their educational histories, their occupations, their husbands' occupations, and their incomes were different in several respects from the patterns of the Seven Sisters' college alumnae.

Educational Histories. With respect to some aspects of their education, graduates of the two colleges were quite similar. They finished post-college education at similar ages (e.g., at age 39 for the coeducational class of 1949 and at age 37 for the women's college class of 1949). A similar percentage majored in the social sciences (26 percent at the women's college compared with 23 percent at Oberlin), although more women's college alumnae majored in such "male" fields as economics and political science (7 percent vs. 2 percent in economics and 7 percent vs. 5 percent in political science). But other aspects of the two groups' educational histories were notably different. Half again as many of the Oberlin graduates received postgraduate fellowships (12 percent vs. 8 percent). A significantly larger proportion of the coed graduates received postgraduate degrees (59 percent vs. 51 percent). The proportion receiving Ph.D.s or major professional degrees in law or medicine was almost exactly the same for the two colleges (approximately 14 percent, but

Table 3. Average age at marriage among coeducational and women's college alumnae, 1934–69, employed in 1982

Class Groups	Coed	Women's
1934	28.4	25.2
1939	26.2	25.7
1944	25.4	24.4
1949	25.4	24.5
1954	24.6	23.9
1959	24.2	23.0
1964	24.7	23.8
1969	25.3	25.0
Average age at marriage	25.5	24.4

Table 4. Average number of children among coeducational and women's college alumnae, 1934–69, employed in 1982

Class Groups	Coed	Women's
1934	1.9	2.2
1939	2.2	2.5
1944	2.7	2.9
1949	2.4	2.8
1954	2.4	2.6
1959	1.8	2.4
1964	1.4	1.7
1969	0.8	0.9

noticeably more of the Oberlin graduates received masters degrees (45 percent vs. 37 percent).

Occupational Histories. Likewise in occupational fields there were striking similarities as well as differences. The proportions of graduates of the two colleges were almost identical in the fields of education (25 percent), social sciences (7 percent), and the professions (10 percent). But there were significantly more graduates of the women's college in business and government (32 vs. 21 percent). Conversely, many more Oberlin graduates were technicians (18 percent vs. 4 percent).

Husbands' occupations showed less similarity than difference between the two colleges. Only engineers and scientists were equally represented in the two groups (15 percent). In general the husbands of the women's college graduates were almost twice as numerous in business and government (35 vs. 19 percent) and were more heavily represented in the professions (25 percent vs. 18 percent). The husbands of Oberlin alumnae, on the other hand, were much more heavily represented among educators (18 vs. 10 percent), and among technicians (10 vs. 2 percent). Overall, an impression emerges that although they possess fewer advanced degrees and come from families with less professional education, the women's college graduates are more affluent. They have married somewhat different types of husbands and have attained a slightly more comfortable standard of living. Their current higher socioeconomic status is possibly correlated with their somewhat lower rates of current employment. In a comparsion of total household income in 1982, the following income differences emerge: 50 percent of the women's college graduates compared with 54 percent of the Oberlin graduates had incomes under $35,000. But 27 percent of the women's college graduates had total household incomes over $75,000 compared with 12 percent of the Oberlin graduates.

Value Differences. Do differences in affluence reflect differences in women's life patterns? Not necessarily, but there are differences in values and attitudes toward women's roles and the household division of labor that correlate with the somewhat more traditional and affluent image of the women's college graduates in comparison with the Oberlin graduates. When asked what is the ideal division of labor in the home, the Oberlin women gave somewhat more egalitarian answers than the graduates of the Seven Sisters school. Respondents were given a choice along a continuum ranging from the idea that the wife should be primarily responsible for the household to the idea that the husband and wife should share the household tasks equally; 75 percent of the Oberlin graduates chose the egalitarian solution compared with 66 percent of the women's college graduates.

These complex results permit the long-standing proponents of coeducation to claim superiority of their system in attracting women students who are a bit more likely to go on to graduate education and to remain in the labor force. But the advocates of women's education can still point to a larger proportion of graduates who majored in traditionally male fields such as economics and who work in business and government. Clearly each college is a small subcultural milieu that attracts somewhat different students from different types of families. Each college exposes women students to a somewhat different educational environment and turns them out into a world where they will forge slightly different lives after graduation.

Yet in overall life patterns, the graduates of the two colleges are more similar than different. Age group differences in past history and present concerns are much more impressive than the relatively minor variations that distinguish the coed and women's college graduates.

AGE GROUP DIFFERENCES

Up to this point my comparisons of the two colleges have lumped together all the responses of the classes of 1934 through 1979, and have revealed small quantitative differences in educational, family, and career histories. When the responses are examined by age of the graduates, however, some very powerful generational differences emerge that are shared by the women regardless of the college they attended. Profiles of the older, middle-aged, and younger women show the contrasts in their past and present lives.[5] One of the open-ended questions in the Life Patterns Survey invited the women to tell whether there was something learned after college for which they wished college had prepared them. Another question elicited information about activities not covered in the survey. A great variety of responses resulted: some proud, some angry; others sad, reflective, or bursting with accomplishments. But three major themes stand out that are associated with era of graduation: (1) the acceptance of the traditional homemaker role among the classes who were graduated during World War II; (2) conflict over career and family in the classes of the late 1950s and early 1960s; and (3) the subordination of personal and family life to career aspiration in the classes of the 1970s. The examples given here come only from Oberlin, but they were duplicated many times by women of similar age from the Seven Sisters college.

The overwhelming story from the class of 1944 was the reality of war and what it meant for the timing and events of women's lives. Being in college had a special meaning when the men were away and the whole country was straining to meet the national emergency. As young women, many waited for their young men to come back. Some married, settled down, and made compromises in their initial career aspirations that they now regret; others devoted themselves to home and community in a way that they would not change.

The following account comes from an Oberlin graduate of 1944 who, if she now could, would change her whole life course:

> My college experiences were atypical, for World War II began during my sophomore year and the coeducational college became largely female. Added to the usual value in those days of finding a husband at college was the urgency of the war, and the need thereafter for the husband to get his education right away to prepare for a profession. I willingly worked so that he could go to school—and by today's standards am very sorry I spent all my time on his needs (and what I perceived as "our" goals) and none on my own. When I was divorced in 1958 and out looking for a job, I did not consider returning to teaching because I did not like the profession very much. I think I chose it because it was what women did. I found raising a child by myself (and with little financial support) difficult, but it taught me to be more self-sufficient in a hurry!
>
> At age 59 I am just beginning to get glimmers of how to be a career woman—and have strong feelings of having missed the boat!

But another woman, now widowed, of the same college and class of 1944, took a different and more traditional path to which she is still committed.

> Marriage, family, home, and husband-supportive role were and still are, in my opinion, totally fulfilling and rewarding. My college course, with a kindergarten-primary major and an English minor, prepared me to carry out this role for my family far better than any daycare center or private sitter could have done. I feel that all four of our children and my husband benefited from the intellectual stimulation, companionship, continuity, and stability that I gave to their lives.
>
> I did have plans for additional self-fulfillment, volunteer service, and a renewal and revitalization of husband-wife relationship when our youngest child left for college but that was not to be. Had I been privy to the life that was to be for us now, in our golden years, I would still have chosen the same career.

Members of the peacetime class of 1959 faced a different world, which was quiet and stable by comparison. The college youth of the 1950s have been called the silent generation. How did the young women from this era fare in 1982? One central thread running through their lives was the struggle to combine career and family. One coed graduate, a teacher until she was 32, left teaching to have four children and is now studying to be a technical writer. She summed up her quest in these terms: "I am struggling to achieve a lifestyle which incorporates physical wellbeing (daily swim or jog or bike), parental responsiveness, ongoing spiritual and intellectual growth, career, and time with husband and friends. Can it be done? I believe so but I'm still (and probably always will be) grappling with how."

While some 45-year-olds expressed excitement and a sense of challenge in combining many aspects of an interesting life, many others referred to missed opportunities. They had early accepted the image of the dependent wife, then encountered difficulties in their marriages and tried to catch up with careers later on. One divorced member of the Oberlin class of 1959 said of herself, "I span the generation which either went from old ideas to new ways of living, or got left behind." To her, "Divorce entailed the trade-off between dependence/security and the chance to grow, emerge, and really live."

Other women spoke of the positive effect on them of changes in society between the 1950s and 1980s. Their divorces and career changes are described in terms of liberation and new opportunity that is less frequent in the stories of older women. One 1959 Oberlin graduate recounts such experiences in the following upbeat way.

> The women's movement has been an integral part of my growth, not because of my own involvement but because of the societal changes which have made opportunities open to me.
>
> My REAL education began three years ago when I was forced to independence by divorce. I had always been "cared for"—by parents, older brothers, spouse—with the ability to rely on others to make economic, political, career, and social decisions. With parents dead, brother dead, and spouse departed, I had to assume responsibilities. Though traumatic, the experience was worth the pay-offs—independence and freedom.

Those who graduated in 1974 also expressed the career-family concerns, but with a relatively greater emphasis on career than on intimate relationships. At a point in their lives when an earlier generation would already have been married for several years, many of the class of 1974 were in 1982 still engaged in career training and were just beginning to think about rounding out the personal side of their lives. One 1974 graduate described her experience working in a nonprofit organization for six years on women's issues and being exposed to American and foreign leaders who were working on women's issues in government, trade unions, universities, and volunteer associations. She wrote in 1982:

I am now taking leave of the paid, "plush" world of philanthropy to pursue a graduate degree in public and private management. My hope is that new credentials, skills, and confidence will serve me better as I continue to work on ways to make people's lives easier and more justly spent.

The last six years have been so busy in personal and professional growth (sometimes just holding on in periods of discouragement or illness) that I have not participated in many intimate relationships with men. As I am coming to like and respect myself more than in the past, I look forward to developing that personal dimension of my life.

Another 1974 graduate shifted from the arts to medicine and is now single-mindedly pursuing her goal of becoming a doctor. Unlike many of the respondents of earlier generations, she is unambivalently oriented to a career. Her personal life comes later:

I would not be involved in the medical profession if not for the Women's Rights Movement and its impact on me during my college years. I grew up in a very conservative traditional environment in which male and female roles were fixed and set even if Mom was unhappy about it. During my college years I rethought all my values and decided I could make my own life different, daring to choose a profession in the traditionally "male" field of medicine. I was lucky and surprised to find encouragement and support from my parents in this decision, and I was able to complete pre-med and medical studies with a minimum of hardship after graduating from college. I am finally beginning to see the end of my training approaching along with my 30th birthday. I wish I were a few years younger to begin this career, but I needed the few extra years it has taken me to integrate the changes over the years (from artist to physician). I now feel enriched by both the artistic training and my career choice. Next I will attempt to arrange my personal/ marital life in a satisfying way and coordinate all three.

When the differences in life patterns are summarized across the three different age groups, it is apparent that more of the older women made an either–or choice between family and career, whereas the younger women were much more likely to believe that they could have it all. Of course, one possibility is that if the class of 1944 had been surveyed when they were age 30, the similarities with the class of 1974 might have been greater; the 55-to-60-year-olds when they were younger might have been more oriented to doing everything. But the internal evidence from the questionnaire casts doubt on this conjecture. The respondents themselves so often refer to the change in the times, to the women's movement, and to expanded opportunities that have influenced their lives that one is convinced that women college graduates' outlooks did change between the 1940s and 1980s and influenced their lives accordingly.

One way of examining the change in life patterns across the decades is to compare the relative frequency of different patterns in each class. The one disadvantage of this method is that younger women's life-course decisions are still in process and are not therefore exactly comparable in 1982 with the patterns visible among older women. Such a procedure nevertheless allows comparison of life patterns of coeducational and women's college graduates; and with caution, comparison can be made across age groups.

In my earlier research on Wellesley College alumnae of the classes of 1911–60, I classified women's life patterns according to a typology of twelve role combinations based on: (1) graduate training, (2) marriage, (3) childbearing, and (4) employment.[6] Only eight of these logical types were found with any frequency in women's actual lives. In the 1982 survey, the overall distributions were very similar for both the coeducational and women's colleges (as shown in Figure 1).

For Oberlin, the coeducational college, by far the largest numbers of graduates were in Life Pattern Type 1, having graduate training, being married, having children, and being employed (35 percent). Type 3 was the second most common pattern (22 percent) and was the same as Type 1 in the role components except that graduate training was lacking. The distribution was a bit different among the women's college alumnae. There Types 1 and 3 were tied for first place (each with 32 percent). Instead of the eight patterns found among the 1911–60 generations of college women, however, the coed and women's college graduates in the 1982 Life Patterns Study exhibited only six or seven patterns. The people with education beyond college who were not in the labor force (Type 2) had become almost nonexistent. But the people who had combined some form of family and career life (Types 1 and 3) held steady at almost 60 percent beginning with the classes of the 1920s.

The pattern of having postgraduate education, marriage, children, and employment began to increase in the classes of the 1930s (as shown in Figure 2). Although the graduates of the coed college were slightly earlier in adopting this pattern, the overall trend for the coed and women's colleges was very similar, rising in the classes that graduated after World War II, then becoming strikingly less apparent in the younger classes of the 1970s, where many members are still single. It is likely that as the younger classes age, more of them will also fall into the Type 1 life

Figure 1. Distribution of Life Pattern Types of Alumnae of Coeducational,
Seven Sisters, and Wellesley Colleges, 1911-79

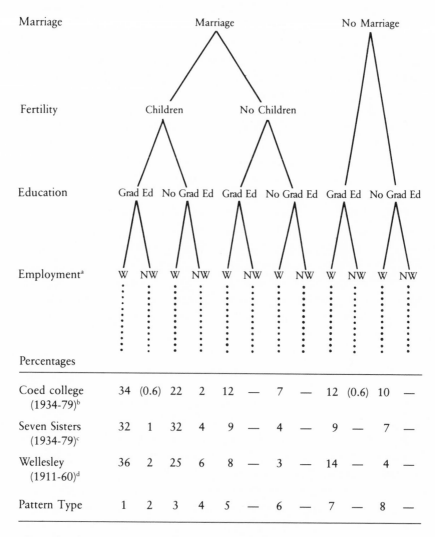

	Grad Ed	No Grad Ed	Grad Ed	No Grad Ed	Grad Ed	No Grad Ed
	W NW	W NW	W NW	W NW	W NW	W NW
Coed college (1934-79)[b]	34 (0.6)	22 2	12 —	7 —	12 (0.6)	10 —
Seven Sisters (1934-79)[c]	32 1	32 4	9 —	4 —	9 —	7 —
Wellesley (1911-60)[d]	36 2	25 6	8 —	3 —	14 —	4 —
Pattern Type	1 2	3 4	5 —	6 —	7 —	8 —

[a]W: employed since graduation; NW: not employed since graduation.
[b]N = 977.
[c]N = 1,269.
[d]N = 12,666.

Figure 2. Age Distribution of Pattern Type 1, Alumnae of Coeducational and Seven Sisters Colleges, 1934-74

Percent Employed

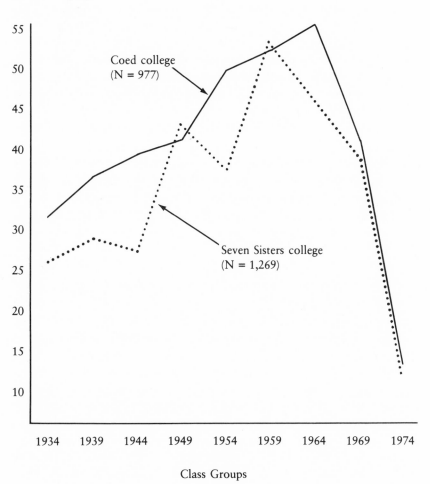

Class Groups

Source: Author's Life Patterns Study Project, 1982.

pattern, but it is also possible that a slightly larger proportion of the classes of the 1970s will always remain single (Type 7 and Type 8).

These age comparisons across the colleges do indeed suggest that coeducation versus single-sex education is a subsidiary issue in a much larger and more powerful current: the changing roles of college-educated women. Whether women are educated alone or with men apparently gives few differential advantages to women who attend one type of college or another. In 1982, the Life Patterns Study found that more graduates of a selective coeducational college had graduate degrees and were in the labor force. But more of the women's college graduates were in "male" fields and were married and had children. Across the classes of 1934 to 1979 the Oberlin graduates adopted the combined family-career pattern somewhat earlier. But the overall distribution of Life Pattern types was very similar among the Oberlin and Seven Sisters graduates both in numbers and timing.

In the nineteenth century both coeducational colleges and women's colleges were pioneers on behalf of women's higher education. In the twentieth century the Oberlin graduates in our survey were some of the earliest to combine work and family life, but the graduates of the Seven Sisters college were not far behind. Despite the small and consistent differences that we found among the graduates of the two colleges in their educational and employment histories, there was an overwhelming similarity in the life patterns of the women who graduated in wartime compared with those who graduated in the 1950s or the 1970s, regardless of the college they attended. These findings put the coeducation-vs.-women's-education debate in its proper perspective. Along with the type of college environment that young women experience in late adolescence and early adulthood, their family background and general economic and social conditions in the larger society will continue to be powerful forces in shaping their lives.

NOTES

Support for the research reported here is from a grant by the National Institute on Aging, 1984–87, to study "Life Course Patterns and Well-Being in Educated Women," Janet Z. Giele, Principal Investigator, and Margie E. Lachman, Co-principal Investigator. Initial support to analyze the 1962 Wellesley Alumnae Survey was provided by a grant from the Lilly Endowment, Inc., to Brandeis University in 1981–83 to study "College Women's Changing Life Patterns,

1900–1980," Janet Z. Giele, Brandeis University, Principal Investigator; Pamela J. Perun, Wellesley College, Co-principal Investigator.

1. Comparison of black and white women's careers and life patterns was also of interest. The study design included a black women's college as well as the Seven Sisters college and the small selective coeducational college.

2. For an account of modern coeducation and single-sex education, see Christopher Jencks and David Riesman, *The Academic Revolution* (Garden City, N.Y.: Doubleday, 1968); also Pepper Schwartz and Janet Lever, "Women in the Male World of Higher Education," in A. S. Rossi and A. Calderwood, eds., *Academic Women on the Move* (New York: Russell Sage Foundation, 1973).

3. M. Elizabeth Tidball, "Perspective on Academic Women and Affirmative Action," *Educational Record* 54 (1973): 130–35; and M. Elizabeth Tidball and Vera Kistiakowsky, "Baccalaureate Origins of American Scientists and Scholars," *Science* 193 (August 20, 1976): 646–52.

4. Mary J. Oates and Susan Williamson, "Women's Colleges and Women Achievers," *Signs* 3 (1978): 795–806.

5. In order to protect the anonymity of the respondents, several occupational and background details have been slightly altered in the responses that are quoted.

6. Janet Zollinger Giele, "Cohort Variation in Life Patterns of Educated Women, 1911–1960," *Western Sociological Review* 13 (1982): 1–24; Pamela J. Perun and Janet Z. Giele, "Life after College: Historical Links between Women's Education and Women's Work," in P. J. Perun, ed., *The Undergraduate Woman: Issues in Educational Equity* (Lexington, Mass.: Lexington Books, 1982).

IV
How Equal Is "Equal Education"?
Gender, Race, and Discrimination

The four essays in this section explore areas in which difficulties and barriers to truly equitable education have proved particularly persistent. The authors ask readers to think critically about the meanings of equity and equality for students, teachers, staff, and administrators in the academy today. In her essay, "The Classroom Climate, Still a Chilly One for Women," Bernice Sandler provides a guide to the ways in which occasionally blatant, but more often subtle, messages of inferiority are communicated to women students, finding such inequities all too common even among those with the best of intentions. Mirra Komarovsky's fine analysis, "College Men: Gender Roles in Transition," investigates the difficulties of contemporary male students in adjusting to the expectations of women students who, having achieved access to elite college education, assume that they will pursue equally demanding academic and professional careers. In "How Equal Is Equal Education: Race, Class, and Gender" Margaret Wilkerson explores the complex situation facing black students and the seemingly endemic discrimination that persists despite substantial efforts to promote racially integrated higher education. In carefully analyzing the interrelated factors of sexism and paternalism, Wilkerson finds that even for the few who attain access to educational opportunity, institutions too often still fail to provide truly equal education for minority students, and particularly black women. Finally, "The Issue of Sexual Preference on College Campuses: Retrospect and Prospect," by John D'Emilio, introduces the problems faced by gay men and lesbians who have attained access to the academy, but only at the cost of disguising their identities. As a group, these essays remind us that the open door of coeducation is not a substitute for engagement in the larger struggle for equality and social justice. And, each author notes, educational institutions have a very special role to play in changing the power relations in society. It is not enough merely to follow contemporary practices; the academy must provide models and guidance.

The Classroom Climate:
Still a Chilly One for Women

BERNICE RESNICK SANDLER

Although many overt barriers have fallen during the last decade so that the door to higher education is now open for women, there are many subtle barriers that still remain—barriers that may be almost invisible to both students and faculty. Indeed, both students and faculty may be completely unaware that anything different is occurring. Yet faculty—men and women alike—often inadvertently treat men and women students *differently* and thereby subtly undermine women's confidence in their academic ability, lower their academic and occupational aspirations, inhibit their learning, and generally lower their self-esteem.

My study of these barriers and this differential treatment grew out of my own personal experiences. A few years ago I attended a seminar for executives at the Aspen Institute in Colorado. There were nineteen people there, four of us female; it was the largest number of women they had ever had. After a few days, I began to realize that the women were getting interrupted quite a bit. I did not want to appear paranoid, so I asked the other women whether or not they had noticed the interruptions. They agreed with my observation. But because of my training in research, and because I wanted to be absolutely sure, I made a table showing the number of male interruptors, male interruptees, female interruptors and female interruptees. The next morning I did not participate but merely observed the seminar and collected data. It turned out that the remaining three women had approximately *double* the number of interruptions compared to the remaining fifteen men. There was also a difference in the kind of interruption for men and women. The interruptions of the men's discourse were really a continuation or development of their comments, such as, "What you are saying is that Confucius and Marx were not very far apart." The interruptions of the women's comments were of a very different nature; they tended to be trivial and unrelated to the women's comments. For example, one woman's husband, a reporter for *The New York Times,* was attending the conference as a spouse. One interruption of her speech consisted of, "Well, what do you think [your husband] would say about that?" This interruption subtly or not so subtly communicated to her that what she had said was not quite as worthwhile as what other people (the men) had said.

I showed my table to the two male co-leaders after the session and tried to convey the information as pleasantly as possible, without a confrontation and with a smile. The men denied the accuracy of my data and insisted I had surely misunderstood; but the next morning there were *no* interruptions of any kind for the women. In other words, the behavior—interrupting—was changeable. To me this meant it was time to write a paper on the subject with the hope of changing other people's behavior.

Under a grant from the Fund for the Improvement of Post-Secondary Education (FIPSE), our Project on the Status and Education of Women began to examine our own extensive files and the literature about differential behavior, and to identify how men and women students are treated differently. We gradually came to realize that many of the so-called problems of women may indeed be related *in part* to how they are treated in the classroom.[1] Let me list some of these problems.

— Women are seen as passive and may often act that way.
— Women do not participate in class as much as men.
— Despite an increase in the number of women in fields such as medicine and law, most women still major in the traditionally female fields, which perpetuate sex segregation in the workplace and perpetuate the occupational ghetto where women earn less money.
— Some women experience a decline in their academic aspirations during their college years.

We looked at two kinds of behaviors: how women are singled out and treated differently, and how women are ignored.

The behaviors I describe and explore are not limited to men. Often women faculty engage in the same behaviors. Even faculty who are most concerned about discrimination may inadvertently and unknowingly treat men and women differently.

These behaviors do not happen in every class, nor do they happen all the time, but they happen often enough so that they constitute a pattern. This pattern of behavior dampens women's ambition, lessens their class-room participation, and attacks their self-confidence, so that women's leadership potential is diminished.

To begin with, some behaviors are not subtle at all; there are obvious overt behaviors that are often disparaging. Indeed, we were surprised to find out that there was still a lot of overtly discriminatory behavior in college classrooms.

Overt discriminatory comments on the part of faculty are not only still surprisingly prevalent but these comments are also often intentional; perhaps those teachers who engage in them are unaware of their poten-tial to do real harm. Such comments may occur not only in individual student-teacher exchanges, but also in classrooms, office consultations, academic advising situations, and other learning contexts.[2] Further, there are some indications that overtly sexist verbal behavior on the part of faculty may be most concentrated in those fields and institutions where women are relative newcomers, and that it often increases in both inten-sity and effect at the graduate level. All of the quotations and examples below are real. All of these examples were culled from recent reports and research, all from within the last few years.

> In other classes they hear women described as "fat housewives," "dumb blondes," as physically "dirty," as "broads," "chicks," or "dames," de-pending on the age of the speaker.[3]

> Class time is taken up by some professors with dirty jokes which . . . often happen to be derogatory to women (i.e., referring to a woman by a part of her anatomy, portraying women in jokes as simple-minded or teases, show-ing women as part of the "decoration" on a slide.)[4]

The invidious nature of such comments can perhaps best be un-derstood by comparing them to similar racial remarks. Few, if any, professors would now make disparaging comments about a black's "seriousness of purpose" or "academic commitment," or use racist humor as a classroom device. In order to experience the derogatory nature of such comments, the reader may wish to substitute the word "black," or any other minority, in the examples that follow. Here are some categories into which such comments fall:

— *Comments that disparage women in general,* such as habitual references to "busy-body middle-aged women," statements to the effect that "women are no good at anything," or the description of a class constituted solely of women as a "goddam chicken pen."[5]

— *Comments that disparage women's intellectual ability,* such as belittling women's competencies in spatial concepts or math, or making statements in class discussion such as, "Well, you girls probably found this boring," or "You women wouldn't understand this feeling. . . ."[6]

— *Comments that disparage women's seriousness or academic commitment* or both, such as, "I know you're competent, and your thesis advisor knows you're competent. The question in our minds is, are you really serious about what you're doing?" or "You're so cute. I can't see you as a professor of anything."[7]

— *Comments that divert discussion of a woman student's work toward a discussion of her physical attributes or appearance,* such as cutting a student off in mid-sentence to praise her attractiveness, or suggesting that a student's sweater "looks big enough for both of us." Although such comments may seem harmless to some professors, and may even be made with the aim of complimenting the student, they often make women uncomfortable because essentially private matters related primarily to the sex of the student are made to take precedence over the exchange of ideas and information. As one student noted, "I have yet to hear a professor comment on the daily appearance of a male colleague. I have yet to go through a week without some comment pertaining to my appearance."

— *Comments that refer to males as "men" but to females as "girls" or "gals," rather than "women."* This non-parallel terminology implies that women are viewed as similar to children and as less serious and as less capable than men.

— *Comments that rely on sexist humor as a classroom device,* either "innocently" to "spice up a dull subject" or with the conscious or unconscious motive of making women feel uncomfortable. Sexist humor can range from the blatantly sexual, such as a physics lecture in which the effects of a vacuum are shown by changes in the size of a crudely drawn woman's "boobs," or the depiction of women in anatomy teaching slides in *Playboy* centerfold poses, to jokes about dating and about women students waiting to be called by men. Such behavior relies on a certain bad taste (usually depicting women in a sexual context that is typically derogatory) in order to create a lively atmosphere in class.[8]

Although they admit awareness of sex-stereotyping language, many professors often justify their continued use of these labels. Frequently they joke about their continued male chauvinism, as though their admission serves as an exoneration for a continuation of sexism.

Sexual harassment can also have a devastating effect on some women's participation in the classroom and elsewhere.[9] Women have been known to drop or to avoid courses, to change majors, and even to change schools or drop out as a result of sexual harassment. Even when the effect of this behavior is less drastic, sexual harassment, like other overt remarks, tells a woman that she is viewed in *sexual* terms rather than as an individual capable of scholastic and professional achievement; it tells a woman that she is *not* viewed as an individual learner, but as a woman, who like "all women" is of limited intellectual ability, operating out of her appropriate "sphere" and likely to fail.

The subtle behaviors are of a different order. Often neither the professor nor the student may notice that anything special has occurred. Singly, these behaviors may have little effect. But when they occur repeatedly, they give a subtle but powerful message to women: they are not as worthwhile as men nor are they expected to participate fully in class, in college, or in life at large.

The Project on the Status and Education of Women identified close to thirty different kinds of subtle behaviors that give women this kind of message.[10] Here are some examples:

— Faculty make more eye contact with men than with women, so that individual men students are more likely to feel recognized and encouraged to participate in class. After reading our report, one female instructor discovered that when she asked a question, she looked only at her male students, as if only men students were expected to respond.

— Professors are more likely to nod and gesture in response to men's comments and questions than to women's.

— Faculty often assume a position of attentiveness such as leaning forward when men are talking. When women talk, faculty may be inattentive, looking at the clock or shuffling papers.

— Professors may group students according to sex, especially in a way that implies that women students are not as competent as men or do not have equal status with men. Some laboratory teachers insist that there be no all-women laboratory teams because "women can't handle the equipment on their own." Others may group the women together "so that they can help each other," or so that they "don't delay the men."

— Professors may give men detailed instructions about how to complete a particular problem or lab assignment in the expectation they will eventually succeed on their own, but may actually do the assignment for women—or allow them to fail with less instruction.

— Despite the popular notion that in everyday situations women talk more than men, studies[11] show that in formal groups containing men and women,

men talk more often than women;

men talk for longer periods and take more turns at speaking;

men exert more control over the topic of conversation;

men interrupt women much more frequently than women interrupt men; and, as I had noticed at Aspen,

men's interruptions of women more often introduce trivial or inappropriately personal comments that bring the woman's discussion to an end or change its focus.

Not only do men talk more, but what men say often carries more weight. A suggestion made by a man is more likely to be listened to, credited to him, developed in further discussion, and adopted by a group than the same suggestion made by a woman. The difficulty in "being heard" or "having their comments taken seriously" has often been noted by women in professional peer groups and is strikingly similar to those cited by some women college students.

Teachers themselves may inadvertently reinforce women students' "invisibility," or communicate different expectations for women than for men students. Faculty behaviors that can have this effect include but are not limited to the following:[12]

— *Ignoring women students while recognizing men students, even when women clearly volunteer to participate in class.* This pattern may lead individual women students to feel invisible.

— *Calling directly on men students but not on women students.* Male faculty, especially, may tend to call directly on men students significantly more often than on women students, possibly because faculty unconsciously presume men will have more of value to say or will be more eager to speak up. Sometimes, however, faculty may wish to "protect" women students from the "embarrassment" they assume women may feel about speaking in class and thus simply discount them as participants.

— *Calling men students by name more often than women students.* Sometimes faculty are surprised to discover that they know the names of proportionately more men than women students in their classes. Calling a student by name reinforces the student's sense of being recognized as an individual. Students of both sexes should be addressed similarly, last names for both or first names for both. Calling men by last name but women by first name implies that women are not on a par with men as adults or as future professionals.

— *Addressing the class as if no women were present.* Asking a question with "Suppose your wife . . ." or "When you were a boy . . ." discounts women students as potential contributors.

— *"Coaching" men but not women students in working toward a fuller answer by probing for additional elaboration or explanation.* Faculty are more likely to ask men students, for example, "What do you mean by that?"

— *Waiting longer for men than for women to answer a question before going on to another student.* Studies at the elementary school level indicate that teachers tend to give brighter students more time to formulate a response. Thus, interrupting women, giving women less time to answer a question, may subtly communicate that women are not expected to know the answer. Men's silence after a question may be more likely to be perceived as the result of reflection or the effort to formulate an answer, whereas women's silence is attributed to "shyness" or lack of a suitable response.

— *Asking women students lower-order questions that require factual answers while asking men higher-order questions that demand personal evaluation and critical thinking.* Such a pattern presumes, and subtly communicates to women students, that they may not be capable of independent thought.

— *Responding more extensively to men's comments than to women's comments.* This pattern may be exacerbated because men students may also be more likely to pay more attention to and pick up on each other's comments, but to overlook those made by women. Thus, male

students may receive far more reinforcement than women for intellectual participation.
— *Crediting men's comments to their "author,"* "As Bill pointed out
. . ." but not giving authorship to women's comments.
— *Using classroom examples that reflect stereotyped ideas about men's
and women's social and professional roles,* as when the scientist,
doctor, or accountant is always "he," while the lab assistant, patient,
or secretary is always "she."
— *Using the generic "he" or "man" to represent both men and women.*
Often when a professor is criticized for using the generic "he" or
"man" the professor will label the issue trivial. It makes one wonder:
if the issue is indeed trivial, why is it so difficult for professors and
others to change it?

Why should these behaviors occur? Many behaviors, of course, origi-
nate long before students reach the college classroom, some perhaps as
early as the cradle. Parents treat male and female babies very differently.
For example, they let baby boys cry longer than girls before picking them
up. Parents talk more to girls, and then when girls exhibit more verbal
behavior, we say this is inborn.

Two major hypotheses may explain the differential treatment. One is
differential expectations and perceptions. If we expect girls and women
to be passive and dependent and not interested in math or science, we
may well set up self-fulfilling prophecies. Second, and perhaps underlying
the differential expectations and perceptions, is the devaluation of what
is female. Throughout our society, what women do has been seen as less
valuable than what men do.

There have been numerous experiments in which two groups of subjects rate such items as articles, works of art, and resumés.[13] The name of
the authors are changed for each group; those items ascribed to women
for the first group are ascribed to men for the second group; and those
items ascribed to men for the first group are ascribed to women in the
second group. The results of these experiments are singularly consistent:
if people believe a woman created the item, they rank it lower than if they
believe a male created it. Both men and women consistently devalue
those items ascribed to females. Studies of how women's success is
viewed show a similar pattern: men's success is attributed to talent;
women's success is attributed to luck.

Even when men and women act similarly, their behavior is viewed differently. He is "assertive"; she is "aggressive" or "hostile." He "lost his cool," implying it was an aberration; she's "emotional" or "menopausal." Thus, her behavior is devalued, even when it is the same as his.

So those who believe, perhaps without even knowing it, that women are not as intellectual, not as capable, not as serious as men, may simply ignore women, treat them differently, or view them as peripheral to the classroom, to the college, and to life itself. The classroom is chilly for women because of these behaviors. Add to this the low number of women faculty and the lack of attention to women in the curriculum itself, and indeed one can see that women and men in the same classroom have very different experiences.

These behaviors are not limited only to the classroom. The Project on the Status and Education of Women has published an article examining behaviors that occur outside of the classroom—in housing, student services, and all extracurricular activities.[14] We are also planning a report on the climate for women faculty and administrators, in which we will explore how they too are treated differently.

What can we do about the chilly classroom right now? The project's report addresses institutional or public solutions to the problem and includes approximately 100 recommendations for faculty, administrators, and students.[15] These recommendations fall into four categories:

1. How to increase awareness of the issues;
2. How to institutionalize solutions, such as issuing a policy statement, or incorporating climate issues into faculty and student evaluations and grievance procedures;
3. How to provide direct help to faculty, such as holding workshops or incorporating climate issues into faculty development programs;
4. How to show support, such as providing funds for institutional research or issuing memos from the president or dean about climate issues.

As overt discrimination disappears, we become increasingly aware of its subtle forms and the less obvious barriers to women's development. We also become increasingly aware of the different ways in which men and women view discrimination. Men are more likely to acknowledge and understand overt, intentional discrimination. When overt barriers are dismantled, as when a department chair no longer excludes women from his department, many men assume that the problem of discrimination is thereby solved.

Many women, on the other hand, view discrimination as being more than just the formal overt barriers. They see a whole host of subtle behaviors that have a discriminatory impact. For example, women may view social behavior, such as male faculty always having lunch together, as having a discriminatory effect because women thereby are excluded from informal sources of information and the subsequent opportunity to learn more about their profession. Thus, many men tend to overstate the progress that has been made, and many women tend to *understate* the progress; that is, men think in terms of how far we have come, and women think in terms of how far we have to go.

The subtle barriers—like those that occur in the classroom—will not be eradicated easily, particularly because they occur not only in college classrooms but also in the ordinary relations between men and women. These barriers are the product of perhaps thousands of years of history, and it will take more than our lifetime—perhaps several generations—to eradicate them completely.

Let me close with something that is characteristic of the new mood of women, a "quotation" from a tablet that was discovered, you understand, by an all-woman team of archaeologists, assisted by women staff and women students:

And they shall beat their pots and pans into printing presses,
And weave their cloth into protest banners.
Nations of women shall lift up their voices with nations of other women.
Neither shall they accept discrimination anymore.[16]

Now this may sound apocryphal but I suspect it may yet prove to come from the Book of Prophets. For what women are learning is the politics of change. The campus, the nation, the world will never again be the same.

NOTES

1. The results of this research have been published as a pamphlet. See Roberta M. Hall and Bernice R. Sandler, *The Classroom Climate: A Chilly One for Women?* (Washington, D.C.: Project on the Status and Education of Women, Association of American Colleges, 1982).

2. For further exploration of these issues see Roberta M. Hall and Bernice R. Sandler, *Out of the Classroom: A Chilly Campus Climate for Women?* (Wash-

ington, D.C.: Project on the Status and Education of Women, Association of American Colleges, 1984).

3. Hall and Sandler, *Classroom Climate*, p. 5.

4. Ibid.

5. Ibid., p. 6.

6. Ibid.

7. Ibid.

8. Ibid.

9. See, for example, *Sexual Harrassment: A Hidden Issue* (Washington, D.C.: Project on the Status and Education of Women, Association of American Colleges, 1978).

10. For a fuller description of these behaviors, see Hall and Sandler, *Classroom Climate*, and Hall and Sandler, *Out of the Classroom*.

11. Hall and Sandler, *Classroom Climate*, p. 8.

12. See note 10.

13. For an overview and discussion, see Veronica F. Nieva and Barbara A. Gutek, "Sex Effects on Evaluation," *The Academy of Management Review 5* (1980): 267–76.

14. See Hall and Sandler, *Out of the Classroom*.

15. Hall and Sandler, *Classroom Climate*, pp. 13–17.

16. From a poster by Mary Chagnon, n.d.

College Men: Gender Roles in Transition

MIRRA KOMAROVSKY

Feminine and masculine social roles in contemporary society present a crazy quilt of contradictions. The ideal images of femininity and masculinity, the division of labor between the sexes in the world of work, in the family, and in other institutional sectors, and the ideologies that support them reflect massive inconsistencies. These inconsistencies are caused by the familiar lead-lag pattern of social change, that is, by rapid changes in some and resistances to change in other related elements of the social system.

I shall document this thesis, drawing largely upon my study of college seniors in an Ivy League men's college, published in 1976, *Dilemmas of Masculinity: A Study of College Youth.*[1] Supplementary evidence of masculine role strains is included in my book, *Women in College: Shaping New Feminine Identities,* published in 1985.[2]

One caveat is in order. I have chosen to highlight the current strains in gender roles. This purpose accounts for a certain one-sidedness of the portrayal and a neglect of some positive changes that have taken place in intersexual relationships.

As I look at the current scene from a perspective of the past several decades, I see tremendous changes in some attitudes of undergraduates and no change in others, with the result that ambivalences, intrapsychic and interpersonal conflicts, and anomie (in the sense of new situations as yet undefined by social norms) are rife.

The male seniors of my 1976 study generally expressed a wish for an intellectually rewarding relationship with a woman. Men's ideal woman today is a far cry from the legendary dumb blonde. To be sure, what some men meant by intellectual rapport was having an appreciative listener: "I wouldn't go out with a girl who wasn't quick and perceptive enough to catch an intellectual subtlety," remarked one young senior. But a more typical attitude was expressed by another youth: "I am looking for an intelligent girl who has opinions on politics, social problems—someone I could talk to about things guys talk about."[3]

Despite this typical attitude, a sizeable minority, about one-third of the sample, reported that intellectual insecurity vis-à-vis female friends did constitute for them a source of some stress. The following excerpts from interviews illustrate the views of this troubled third:

"I may be a little frightened of a man who is superior to me in some field of knowledge, but if a girl knows more than I do, I resent her." Again, another commented: "I enjoy talking to more intelligent girls, but I have no desire for a deep relationship with them. I guess I still believe that the man should be more intelligent." And still another senior reported: "Once I was seeing a philosophy major, and we got along quite well. We shared a similar outlook on life, and while we had some divergent opinions, I seemed better able to document my position. One day, by chance, I heard her discussing with another girl an aspect of Kant that just the night before she described to me as obscure and confusing. But now she was explaining it to a girl so clearly and matter-of-factly that I felt sort of hurt and foolish. Perhaps it was immature of me to react this way."[4]

Some men were caught in a double bind. They valued originality and intelligence in female as well as male associates, but they could not relinquish the internalized norm that as men they should enjoy an edge of superiority over women. One senior remarked about his current girlfriend: "I am beginning to feel that she is not bright enough. She never says anything that would make me sit up and say, 'Ah, that's interesting!' I want a girl who has some defined crystal of her own personality and does not merely echo my thoughts." He recently met a girl who fascinated him with her quick and perceptive intelligence but this new girl made him feel "nervous and humble."[5]

Occasionally a man intellectually committed to egalitarian ideals experienced guilt. As one put it: "Tugging at my conscience is the thought that I am really most comfortable in situations where my fragile sense of security is not threatened by a woman."[6]

A similar mix of newer egalitarian and traditional attitudes was revealed with respect to the question: "Are some majors or occupational choices considered unfeminine?" The majority of male seniors in my 1976 study expressed acceptance of pioneering choices on the part of their female friends. One youth remarked that he would be flattered to date a career-oriented woman, adding: "A girl so dedicated to her work must think an awful lot of you if she wants to spend time with you."[7]

But again, there were some voices from the past. A pre-law student confessed: "When I went to take the law boards, I was shocked to see all those girls. I didn't think I would feel that way, but I did. Any girl has to be pretty smart and aggressive to go into this field, and it is a threat to the security of all men in the legal profession."[8]

Another student, having declared his full support for equal opportunities for women in the occupational world, added a qualification: "A woman should not be in a position of firing an employee. It is an unpleasant thing to do. Besides, it is unfair to the man. He may be a very poor employee, but he is still a human being, and it may be just compounding his unhappiness to be fired by a woman."[9]

Some observers might argue that in our competitive society comparative rating, rivalry, and envy are also unavoidable in male-to-male relationships. But there remains an important difference—the normative expectation that in certain specified spheres, although not all, a male must enjoy an extra margin of superiority over a woman. This expectation runs counter to some newer values which modern men also accept.

Such inconsistencies are often unconscious. One liberal senior exclaimed passionately: "There are no unfeminine majors—I admire a coed who is pre-law or pre-med. More power to her." But the same senior in another part of the interview was asked to illustrate what he felt was unfeminine behavior. Well, he answered, contrasting "guys" and "girls," he was turned off by a girl who was too concerned about grades. If a pre-med guy goes to see a professor about a C in chemistry, he doesn't like it, but he understands the guy's anxiety about getting into medical school; however, in a girl he finds such grade-consciousness positively obnoxious. There were other illustrations of sanctioning new goals for women but condemning the means necessary to realize such goals. For example, what male students saw as an acceptable degree of assertiveness in a male student club director, and what they even admired as effective leadership, was occasionally perceived as abrasive and aggressive in a female director.[10]

Nowhere are such unconscious ambivalences more striking than in the attitudes of the seniors toward their future wives' occupational roles. The ethos on the campus of this study clearly demanded a liberal attitude toward working wives. But the interviews revealed that the images of the full-time homemaker and a career wife each contained both attractive and repellent traits.

Deprecating remarks about housewifery were not uncommon, even among men with traditional views of women's roles. A conservative senior declared, "A woman who works is more interesting than a housewife." "If I were a woman," remarked another senior, "I would want a career. It must be boring sitting around the house doing the same thing day in, day out. I don't have much respect for the type of woman whom I see doing the detergent commercials on TV."

But the low esteem attached by some of the men to full-time homemaking coexisted with other sentiments and convictions which required just such a pattern for one's wife. For example, asked about the disadvantages of being a woman, one senior replied, "Life ends at 40. The woman raised her children, and all that remains is garden clubs and that sort of thing—unless, of course, she has a profession." In another part of the interview, this young man explained that he enjoyed shyness in a girl and detested aggressive and ambitious women. He could never be attracted to a career woman. It is no exaggeration to conclude that this man could not countenance in a woman who was to be his wife the very qualities that he himself felt were necessary for a fulfilling middle age— for any woman.[12]

An articulate senior illustrates my thesis vividly: "I would not want to marry a woman whose only goal is to become a housewife. This type of woman would not have enough bounce and zest in her. I don't think a girl has much imagination if she just wants to settle down and raise a family from the very beginning. Moreover, I want an independent girl, one who has her own interests and does not always have to depend on me for stimulation and diversion. However, when we both agree to have children, my wife must be the one to raise them. She'll have to forfeit her freedom for the children. I believe that, when a woman wants a child, she must also accept the full responsibility of child care."[13]

To sum up, male attitudes toward working wives included the following contradictions: recognition of the right of an able woman to a career of her choice; admiration for women who measure up in terms of the dominant values of our society; a sense of both the lure and also the threat that such women present; a low valuation attached to housewifery, but the conviction that there is no substitute for the mother's care of young children; and the deeply internalized norm of male occupational superiority pitted against the principle of equal opportunity irrespective of sex.

Such ambivalences on the part of college men tend to exacerbate role conflicts in women. The latter sense that even the men who pay lip service to the creativity of child rearing and domesticity reserve their admiration (if occasionally tinged with ambivalence) for women achievers outside the home.

If men really believed that the rearing of children is more difficult, creative, and significant than writing books or managing corporations, they would demand more of a hand in it too. How telling of our operative values is a report published in *The New York Times* in 1981 citing two male nursery school teachers who in new encounters described themselves as "school" rather than nursery school teachers.

I have stressed masculine ambivalences. But my 1985 study of women undergraduates reveals that they are caught up in role confusion which in turn creates problems for their male associates. To pick out a random illustration, some women were emotionally attracted to macho men who "took charge of things," but such men were not likely to satisfy their equally strong expectations for egalitarian rather than traditional female-male relationships.

What of the future?

I cannot conceive of a utopian society in which human beings could be completely free of painful dilemmas, incompatible goals, regret, jealousy, or frustrations. The problems I have just illustrated do not fall, in my opinion, into the category of those intrinsic to the human condition. I consider the difficulties I have cited as social problems, that is, potentially remediable difficulties stemming from the lead-lag character of social change.

To illustrate this point, I turn to my recent study, in which female freshmen filled out an adjective checklist for "My Ideal Man." They frequently checked such expressive attributes as sensitive, warm, affectionate, and the like. In one case, a boyfriend, looking over the checked qualities, exclaimed, "But you are describing a woman, not a man. What you want is a sister."[14]

This young man, and to an extent all of us, are in trouble because we are caught on the horns of a false dilemma—not having the imagination to realize that there is a third option. The only alternative that came to the young man's mind when traditional gender roles were challenged was simple reversal. I could almost hear him say: "If I am not the one to tell her, 'rely on me, I'll be brave and strong,' must I then say, 'I'll rely on you?' If the husband is not going to be the mainstay, the leader, the dominant partner—will the wife then be the boss? If women are not to be reared to be loving, warm, supportive, will they be hard, competitive and aggressive?"

But are courage and warmth, achievement and compassion, moral strength and sensitivity, self-confidence and capacity to love, doing and being—are these antithetical qualities to be neatly allocated to each sex? Must we not, instead, try to rear both little boys and little girls to be warm *and* strong, creative *and* sensitive, able to accept responsibility for themselves and for others? Ideally these are the attributes which, in various degrees, might be combined in all human beings, played out at different times and in different situations.

Models of egalitarian sexual relationships, especially in marriage, were simply not available in reality or in literature on a scale to shape the imagination of these students, or free them of the false dilemma of power. A clearer insight into the possibility of complementary strengths and weaknesses within a marriage was shown, in an earlier study, by a twenty-eight-year-old taxi driver with nine years of schooling. Asked who was the boss in his family, he answered: "It is hard to say. We go to pieces differently. She's like a powerful engine that shakes itself to pieces. I'm likely to run down. I make her calm down and she makes me stick together."[15]

We need to present to both men and women more vivid models of egalitarian relationships between the sexes in order to replace the traditional ones so deeply etched in social consciousness. But the agenda for needed reforms is far broader and more radical than consciousness-raising. In order to translate pious egalitarian pronouncements about wider and more equal options for men and women into a new reality, we shall have to reorganize several institutions in a far more profound way, in my opinion, than would be necessary, for example, to solve the problems of the black minority in the United States. For example, we Americans are vociferous about the sanctity and centrality of the family, even as we grant every other major institution a prior claim to pursue its interest without the slightest concession to family welfare. The public takes it for granted that the industrial time clock is not to be tampered with, no matter what the consequences are for children and families. A recent survey of many top American companies showed that only about one-third offer some flexible work hours, only 4 percent have policies aimed to help the spouse of a relocating employee to find a job, and only 19 percent offer monetary support for child-care facilities.[16]

Strong social movements are necessary to mediate between intolerable conditions and social remedies. What better proof is needed than a comparison of public nurseries in Britain and Sweden, provided in a study by Mary Ruggie? The unprecedented increase in paid employment of mothers with young children in Britain failed to generate enlightened policies with regard to nursery schools. By contrast, in Sweden the coalition of government, business, and labor resulted in the commitment of the state to cope with the consequences of the entry of women into the labor force.

The social reorganization to be brought about by political and social movements and public policies is too complex a subject to be treated in this discussion. The necessary radical changes will take time. There is no gainsaying the pessimistic short-range outlook, for reasons obvious to us all. But the long-range outlook is a different story.

The demographic, economic, and cultural trends that are changing the status of women are not likely to be reversed. Even in an irrational society fraught with vested interests and fearful resistance to new values, there does exist a strain toward consistency. In a society such as ours, in which the proportion of married women in the labor force exceeds 50 percent, in which over half of college freshmen are women, in which the fertility rate stands at a low 1.9 children per woman, in such a society the persistence of traditional sex roles will continue to cause such stress and contradictions as to generate, I believe, over the long run, an irresistible pressure for necessary social reorganization in the direction of sex equality. Our society must become one in which neither sex is the "second sex."

NOTES

1. Mirra Komarovsky, *Dilemmas of Masculinity: A Study of College Youth* (New York: W. W. Norton, 1976).

2. Mirra Komarovsky, *Women in College: Shaping New Feminine Identities* (New York: Basic Books, 1985).

3. Komarovsky, *Masculinity,* p. 47.

4. Ibid., p. 49.

5. Ibid., p. 50.

6. Ibid., p. 131.

7. Ibid., p. 25.

8. Ibid., p. 26.

9. Ibid., p. 36.

10. Ibid., p. 27.

11. Ibid., p. 35.

12. Idem.

13. Ibid., p. 38.

14. Komarovsky, *Women,* p. 245.

15. Mirra Komarovsky, *Blue Collar Marriage* (New York: Random House/Vintage Books, 1967), p. 179.

16. Komarovsky, *Women,* pp. 317–18.

17. Mary Ruggie, *The State and Working Women* (Princeton, N.J.: Princeton University Press, 1984).

How Equal Is Equal Education: Race, Class, and Gender

MARGARET B. WILKERSON

Equal education has never been a priority item on the public agenda of our nation. In the best of times, it has been included with reluctance, and then only after great pressure was brought to bear through legislation, court action, or civic disturbance. What progress has been made has been both limited and uneven—and seemingly possible only during periods of economic growth and expansion. Now, as fiscal retrenchment occurs in our troubled economy, equal education is viewed as an unaffordable luxury and, in some minds, a threat to quality.

A fundamental problem is the interpretation of the term "equal education" and the actions it implies. In practice, the term has meant that certain "others" largely left out of educational opportunities must or should now be included according to various formulas: in proportion to the percentage of whites in higher education, or perhaps in proportion to the number of minorities in the population, or a particular percentage of high school graduates, or according to some other goal or quota. Policies imply a condescending attitude: Let them inside the door; let the least different among them sit next to these privileged others so that they, too, can benefit from the opportunities of higher education. Thus the primary thrust in seeking equal education for the past several decades has been *access*. And, indeed, it has been a proper first step.

According to a panel of educators convened by the Fund for the Improvement of Post-Secondary Education (FIPSE), access is the single most important change and improvement in higher education over the past decade for all groups formerly excluded or underrepresented. In fact, the panel, of which I was a member, was itself representative of the winds of change which have wafted (not "swept," unfortunately) through the hallowed halls of ivy; the panel composition was diverse by ethnicity and gender, by role and relation to the higher educational community, and by type of institution. The FIPSE Panel found that the increased number of women, mature learners, and to a lesser extent, minorities entering colleges and universities has caused sweeping changes in some institutions and the creation of some new ones. The majority of students in our nation's colleges are women. Minorities now have greater access to higher education than ever before. These "new" students have driven some colleges to rethink their mission, to revise their curricula, to introduce new and innovative programs, to initiate sounder evaluation methods, and, in some cases, to change the composition of their work-force. The triple whammy of the Civil Rights Movement, student activism of the 1960s and early 1970s, and the Women's Movement has indeed changed the student and employee population of many of our institutions.

How much change has occurred, and how lasting is it likely to be? A 1979 report of the National Forum on Learning in the American Future, which addressed future needs and goals for adult learning from 1980 to the year 2000, indicated that the gains may be temporary and that higher education has already begun to subordinate minority issues to other concerns. Respondents to this survey, who included 1,556 policy decision makers, educators, and scholars, ranked minority issues low among future goals.[1] *The Final Report of the Commission on the Higher Education of Minorities,* prepared by a blue-ribbon panel convened by the Ford Foundation, noted further evidence of the cooling trend. "If the current attitude of some educators toward minority issues is one of benign neglect or indifference, the attitudes expressed by some litigants through the federal courts may be characterized as overtly hostile. The U.S. Supreme Court's DeFunis (1974) and Bakke (1978) cases, for example, reflect a growing public view that higher education institutions have 'gone too far' in their attempts to accommodate the special needs of minorities."[2]

The dramatic gains made by women, particularly white women, illustrate the persistence and perniciousness of barriers to equal education for both women and men of color, and for the poor. While numbers of white women of middle and upper income levels continue to rise (though at a slightly slower pace than before) at each level of education and degree attainment, blacks, Hispanics, Puerto Ricans and Native Americans are increasingly underrepresented at each level; these minority groups have greater-than-average attrition rates from all levels and disproportionately high losses in the transition from high school to college. Studies also show that parental income alone predicts persistence and achievement for all four minority groups, but is unrelated to the college performance of whites. After dramatic increases in the 1960s, few gains in the numbers of minorities admitted to institutions of higher education have been made since the mid-1970s. Blacks, who can be used as a gauge of the progress of other ethnic minorities, are declining in number and proportion enrolled in graduate and professional schools. Although their numbers have increased in business, engineering, and the sciences, blacks continue to be underrepresented, constituting fewer than 2 percent of the recent graduates in those fields. Although the number of blacks receiving doctoral degrees doubled from 581 to 1,055 between 1973 and 1979, blacks still receive no more than 4 percent of all professional and doctoral degrees. Three out of four of those degrees are in the overcrowded fields of education and the social sciences, where salaries are the lowest and unemployment rates highest. The representation of blacks on faculties of predominantly white institutions hovers at approximately 1 to 2 percent and less than that for Hispanic-Latinos and Native Americans. As minorities cluster in two-year colleges and thus are less likely to move on to four-year colleges, there is serious doubt that they are receiving an equal education. Cuts in financial aid to students along with the rise in college costs further reduce the number of minorities and poor who can afford a college education or who are financially able to move into four-year institutions.[3]

The prognosis for the future is troubling as the quality of secondary education for minorities deteriorates in many areas. In 1954, the *Brown* v. *Board of Education* landmark decision sought to effect equality of education in the nation's schools. Now, more than thirty years later, we find racial segregation in the schools on the rise. The Orfield report from the Joint Center for Political Studies, which examined trends in the fifty largest urban school districts and forty-four metropolitan areas, including suburbs, showed that in 1980 two-thirds of the students in the ten largest school districts belonged to minorities, and the ratio is rising rapidly. School districts that tested voluntary desegregation showed no improvement in segregation levels from 1968 to 1980. School districts that made the most substantial progress in the past fifteen years had extensive court-ordered busing programs that integrated suburban and city children, most of them in the South. However, recent legal challenges to busing programs have greatly diminished reliance on this strategy. In urban areas, the rise in minority populations and decrease in white populations are turning schools into involuntary "minority institutions," overcrowded, understaffed, poorly or inadequately funded. Thus access, the one area where some progress has been seen, is once more proving to be elusive for minorities.

The issue of equal education does not yield to easy generalizations or quick solutions. For it goes to the heart of our democratic ideals and challenges our claim to be a land with room enough for non-European minorities, for women, and for the poor who are among her citizens. The recipe for equal education apparently has been to add minorities, women, and other excluded groups and to continue to stir as usual. Now we find that it is not so simple, that the presence of these students raises fundamental questions which challenge the assumptions upon which our society and consequently our educational institutions are built.

For white men and women in coeducational settings, the questions of gender roles and stratification, the legacy of sexism and a paternalistic society may be preeminent; but for people of color, racism in its varied forms both subtle and blatant may well be the overriding issue, even for women of color. Before we leap to defend one or the other as the most pervasive factor, let me hastily add that both are strong and interrelated forces, two sides of the same paternalistic coin, which have a disproportionate impact on minorities and on women. The emerging scholarship on racism and sexism, especially the work coming out of southern and western regions, describes a pattern of attitudes and influences that work to render the minority male socially and politically impotent, that is, to place him in a powerless position relative to white males, while encouraging in him a false sense of superiority over women, or at least certain women. The same influences nurture in white women a sense of privilege based on color; this "pedestal syndrome" can be called forth to buttress divisions along racial lines. In a few rare instances, the chimera of brassy minority women will be used against both groups. These patterns are often observed in hiring situations and sometimes in the admissions process, for example, "We did not hire (admit) you because we had to hire (admit) a black or Hispanic woman (man) or a member of another 'protected' group." Within minority groups, the influences of sexism can be seen. For example, sex differences, in choice of major field and in career aspirations, are more pronounced among minorities than among whites. At all degree levels women are more likely to major in allied health fields, the arts and humanities, and education, whereas men are more likely to major in business, engineering, the physical sciences, and mathematics, a pattern particularly pronounced in predominantly white institutions. The twin forces of racism and sexism have their greatest impact on women of color.

What happens when racism is minimized as a factor? If we look at black colleges, we find not only a higher rate of completion, but also that women's degree attainment in all fields is much closer to parity, although some disparities remain. It is worth noting here that there is a higher percentage of women faculty and administrators in black colleges; the legacy of egalitarianism in black culture—slavery made us all equal.

Minority women, however, across all institutions, are heavily concentrated in the field of education; in 1975–76, 8 percent of white women receiving baccalaureates were education majors, in contrast to 24 percent of Hispanic women, 31 percent of black women, and 32 percent of American Indian women. At the master's level in 1978–79, 52 percent of white women, 53 percent of Hispanic women, 57 percent of American Indian women, and 66 percent of black women received their degrees in education. At the doctorate level, approximately one-third of white and Hispanic women, half of American Indian women and two-thirds of black women earned degrees in education. Their choice was related to a number of factors: perception of job opportunities, necessity of working, commitment to "lift as we climb" or to aid the progress of their racial group, and college experiences that drove them from other fields.

Pressure on minority males can be overwhelming. The number of suicides and mental breakdowns among black students at some elite institutions is alarming as minority men and women recognize how rare is their presence, how much rides on their achievement, how visible they are. Often these students do not have the luxury of merely representing themselves; they represent an entire race or group whether they wish to or not. When I went away to college in the 1950s, the whole city of Los Angeles seemed to know. To augment my college scholarship, the Our Authors' Study Club gave me $100, the First A. M. E. Zion Church of which I was a member raised about $50 for me during a church service, and one of my high school teachers enclosed postage stamps in a card of congratulations. All impressed upon me that I was one of "the rare ones" going to a university. My achievement or failure would be theirs as well.

They also knew that the options for an uneducated minority woman or man are few. As the number of minority college entrants diminishes, the pressure on those few to achieve increases proportionately. They become a very precious commodity to their respective communities.

It is important to be cognizant of differences among minority groups, not to blur them into a meaningless whole. For example, enrollment and attrition rates differ among and within minority groups. At the University of California at Berkeley as well as other California campuses, the enrollment of black male students is generally lower than that of black females, although their completion rate is slightly higher. Hispanic men persist at a higher rate than Hispanic women. We are uncertain of the reasons for these differences. A survey of minority educators showed that Chicano, American Indian, and Puerto Rican respondents believed that the greatest strength of their young people is strong cultural identity, whereas blacks felt that black young people are distinguished most by intelligence, curiosity, resilience, and flexibility.[4] There are factors in the educational experience which impact upon men and women of color in very distinct and sometimes disparate ways. These and other differences must be recognized if institutions are to respond adequately. At the same time, in our fad-oriented zeal to embrace gender issues, we should not forget that race itself remains a critical factor. Within the coeducational context, we must be cognizant of the importance of both race and sex in the academic and social lives of our students.

The presumption of inferiority is one of the most persistent barriers to minority achievement. If white women students are often viewed as wives, mothers, homemakers-in-the-making who do not "need" the same educational opportunities as men, what images of minorities are carried in our heads? Are they the maids of those homemakers, the nannies, the janitors, bus drivers and porters, the dumb athletes, the prostitutes, more recently the "affirmative action" slot filled by virtue of court action, not ability? Behind our statements that minorities need "special help" or remediation lurks the suspicion or assumption that they are slow to learn, not that they may approach a subject differently by virtue of experiences or may have been subjected to inferior educational circumstances or poor learning environments. There is a strong tendency to blame the victim, not the institutions that failed him or her.

The issue of equal education raises fundamental questions about our admissions practices for both men and women. How valid, for example, are aptitude tests as predictors of success for minorities? Studies show that motivation and learning environment are more critical. The interview and the personal recommendation are proving to be more valid methods of selecting students who can and will persist. In fact, many colleges are finding that students admitted with low GPAs and low SAT scores (unfortunately called special admits) do, with the proper support and assistance, perform on a par with other students who initially met the regular standards. McGeorge Bundy, former president of the Ford Foundation, raised the question provocatively:

> If I am a qualified black . . . may not my blackness perhaps make me more qualified? Have I had something extra to go through? If I score 550 where a middle-class white scores 650, have I shown as much or more of what is so critical to success in learning—a determination to learn? Can I bring a difference and needed perspective? Is there a special need for people like me in courts and hospitals and on college faculties? May the profession itself be better if more people of my race are in it? Can my presence and participation as a student enlarge the educational experience of others? Does the whole society somehow have a need for me in this profession that it simply does not have, today, for one more white? If the answer to these questions, or some of them, is yes, are not my qualifications by that much improved, and improved precisely by my blackness? If so, at some point it becomes right that I should be admitted; I am not "less qualified" when all things are considered.[5]

Thus the issue of admissions and standards is tied to larger questions about the purpose of education and its responsibility to society.

The surge in the minority student population in the late 1960s brought demands for new programs and departments. Administrators, their backs against ivy-covered walls, responded reluctantly, with various ethnic studies programs. Women's studies came along several years later, carrying the same stigma of political expediency and inferiority. Today, there is an explosion of serious scholarship posing new questions that force a rethinking of traditional Euro-centered, male-centered, class-biased disciplines and that seek to redefine who and what is studied as well as why, and how this knowledge contributes to an understanding of the world. Yet even women's studies must guard against being white female-centered, whereas ethnic studies must work to reflect better the perspectives and experiences of ethnic women. Nevertheless, despite these dangers, both have great potential for transforming traditional disciplines.

Joseph Meeker, an iconoclastic educator and author of an article entitled "Ambidextrous Education or: How Universities Can Come Unskewed and Learn to Live in the Wilderness," suggests that the exclusion of minorities, women, and the poor may have preserved in them a quality desperately needed in higher education today. Following his belief in the distinction between right- and left-brain thinking, Meeker claims that colleges and universities have been dominated by left-brain thinkers—those who think in linear fashion, reading the world page by page and word by word, creating neat and logical specialties—rather than right-brain thinkers, those who prefer synthetic thinking, reading books rather than pages, loving chords rather than melodies, embracing simultaneity, irony, and ambiguity. As Meeker explains:

> The trouble is that education, hooked as it is to linear functions, fails to encourage right-brained weavers. Balanced mentalities are easiest to find among those who have never attended universities or who have recovered from their influence through several years of post-educational living in larger contexts. By denying higher education to some people—women, racial minorities, the poor—we have managed to keep their right brains in working order, even though they may lack status, power, or adequate learning. The left brain's dream of social unity arising from universal higher education has never been realized. That may be the luckiest break we've had in recent centuries. Those who are innocent of universities and those who have convalesced from their effects are perhaps the best hope for the future of higher education.[6]

Tongue-in-cheek, Meeker verges on the romantic while legitimately questioning sacrosanct notions about formal learning.

The "add-and-stir" notion of equal education focuses attention on the deficiencies of the minority or woman or poor student without considering the inadequacies of the institution. As important as academic support programs are for many of these students, the total learning environment is just as critical: institutional expectations of these students; faculty attitudes; the number of female and male minority role models in administrative, faculty, and staff ranks; opportunities to learn about the multicultural heritage of this country; and many other elements that contribute to the intellectual development not only of the minority or woman student, but to the entire student population. By seriously addressing the question of equal education, we can improve the educational experience for women and men students, better addressing learning needs and broadening the narrow view of the world under which both white and minority men and women labor.

The question of equal education goes beyond the narrow perceptions about access. The issues are integral to the purposes of the academy and its relationship to the world. The issues are about the building of knowledge, the use and transmission of information, the breadth of learning, and what is worthy of study. The issues are about access to the marvelous opportunity for learning, the perspectives brought to academe, and the responsibility of academic professions. These are issues for all learners, for all institutions, whether or not they are in the business of education. These questions are intricately linked to our national identity.

We are living in a very troubled society, one that has never reconciled a fundamental conflict between its democratic ideals and its racist, sexist and classist practices. We are virtually surrounded by the evidence: the declining numbers of blacks progressing through our educational system and thus foreshadowing an even smaller pool of candidates for college and university faculties in the future; the growing economic gap between racial minorities and whites; the increased number of women and minority men living in poverty; the flight of middle-class whites along with corporate investors from the "colored" and poor inner cities; the increased segregation of our communities and our schools; the depletion of support for historically black colleges; the continued discrimination against even those who are well educated, to name only a few. And now enter the "new poor," added on to the "old poor," the new ranks of unemployed whose jobs are obsolete as this economy rapidly evolves from postindustrial to high technology. Education is no panacea for these searing social problems. But the educational community does have a responsibility to do more than mirror our society's worst faults. The studies that illuminate the issues and problems exist. The strategies that lead toward solutions are available. A number of publications have addressed the questions well: *The Final Report from the Commission on Higher Education,* the 1981 *Daedalus* issue on minorities, *Minority Access to Higher Education* published by the American Association of Higher Education, the joint publication by the American Council on Education and Ford Foundation entitled *Race and Equity in Higher Education,* and the 1985 report published by the College Board, *Equality and Excellence: The Educational Status of Black Americans.*[7] Part of the wonderful legacy of the decades of increased access is the knowledge that we now possess on achieving equal education. Do we have the will to use it?

Limited as the concept of equal education may be in practice and limited though its progress may be, it has, along with coeducation, opened the door not only to minorities and women, but to a fundamental rethinking of the purposes and practices of education. But it is still a very narrow opening. Educators must take the lead in insisting that our system become truly meritocratic, that we learn to cultivate talent and ability in whatever packaging it appears. Coeducation must make equal education a priority item, the hallmark of a learning experience that better prepares women and men of all races to live together in the New World.

NOTES

1. R. Glover and B. Gross, *Report on the National Forum on Learning in the American Future: Future Needs and Goals for Adult Learning, 1980–2000* (New York: Future Directions for a Learning Society, The College Board, 1979).

2. *Final Report of the Commission on the Higher Education of Minorities* (Los Angeles: Higher Education Research Institute, 1982), p. 9.

3. Ibid., pp. 16–19.

4. Ibid., p. 23.

5. McGeorge Bundy, "The Issue before the Court: Who Gets Ahead in America?" *The Atlantic,* November 1977, p. 48.

6. Joseph Meeker, "Ambidextrous Education or: How Universities Can Come Unskewed and Learn to Live in the Wilderness," *North American Review* 260 (Summer 1975): 41.

7. *Final Report of the Commission on the Higher Education of Minorities* (Los Angeles: Higher Education Research Institute, 1982); *Daedalus: Journal of the American Academy of Arts and Science,* issue title: "American Indians, Blacks, Chicanos, & Puerto Ricans," Spring 1981; Jean L. Preer, *Minority Access to Higher Education,* AAHE-ERIC/Higher Education Research Report No. 1 (Washington, D.C.: American Association for Higher Education, 1981); Reginald Wilson, ed., *Race and Equity in Higher Education* (Washington, D.C.: American Council on Education, 1982); Linda Darling-Hammond, *Equality and Excellence: The Educational Status of Black Americans* (New York: College Board, 1985); see also Office of Minority Concerns, *Minorities in Higher Education* (Washington, D.C., American Council on Education, 1984).

The Issue of Sexual Preference on College Campuses: Retrospect and Prospect

JOHN D'EMILIO

To explore the *recent* history of the sexual preference issue on college campuses is a redundancy; sexual preference as an issue—that is, as something that involves controversy, contention, or debate—has only a recent history. It was as recently as 1967 that the first gay student group was formed on a college campus, and only 1973 when lesbian and gay male faculty, graduate students, and university staff formed the Gay Academic Union.

Discussions of the issue must take account of the critical differences between sexual preference and two other social categories, gender and race, often examined in relation to oppression and inequality. First of all, the body of historical experience is vastly different. We have more than a century of institutional experience to draw upon in looking at issues of gender and racial inequality. That translates into the time to have tried a variety of approaches under changing social conditions, to have refined our strategic perspective, and to be able to assess successes and failures. Gay men and lesbians lack this historical tradition. The first gay rights organization was formed in Los Angeles in 1950, the first lesbian organization in San Francisco in 1955, the first gay student group was chartered at Columbia in 1967, and the first faculty group came into existence in New York City in 1973. One result of the relative poverty of this historical experience is that the agenda for achieving equality remains in many ways unformulated and underdeveloped.

A second critical difference, related to the first yet also distinct, concerns the comparative status of the issue of inequality based on gender, race, and sexual preference. Gender and racial oppression remain pervasive in America; they are systemic and institutionalized. Yet there is also a large body of formal opinion, cultural belief, and law that supports equality in principle and provides some tools for moving toward equality in practice. This is not yet true for lesbians and gay men. Almost half of the states retain criminal penalties for homosexual behavior; only one state, Wisconsin, has added sexual preference to its civil rights laws; and court decisions, while strong in some areas, are weak or nonexistent in others. Courts that routinely deny lesbians custody of their children, for instance, are unlikely to be staunch defenders of the right of gay women and men to teach America's youth.

Finally, equality on the basis of sexual preference is at its heart a question of coming out. Equal access has been a critical issue for racial minorities and for women, but gay men and lesbians are already well represented in the university community. For us a primary mark of equality is not entry to the university but whether, once there, we can come out on campus and still remain on campus.

These differences, and their impact on the situation of gay men and lesbians in the academy, can best be explored by first reviewing briefly the history and then describing the current status of three areas of concern: students, faculty, and scholarship.

STUDENTS

Students have taken the lead in creating a visible gay and lesbian presence in the university community. The first organizational expression of gay political consciousness on a college campus came in 1967, when students at Columbia University formed the Student Homophile League. It says something about the state of American society then that all of the students felt compelled to use pseudonyms. *The New York Times* carried a front-page story about the group, but the nature of its coverage suggests that the *Times* did not consider the event a blow for human freedom.[1]

The gay liberation phase of the homosexual freedom movement began during the summer of 1969 in the wake of the Stonewall Riots in New York City. The police raid of a Greenwich Village gay bar, the Stonewall

Inn, provoked three nights of rioting and led to the rapid proliferation of militant gay organizations. Gay liberation quickly attached itself to the larger radical impulse called "the Movement"—the combination of black power, antiwar activity, countercultural protest, and feminism that occupied American youth in the 1960s. Because so much of the political protest of the sixties was student-based, it was natural that gay liberation would grow on campuses. Lesbian and gay male students benefited from the radicalism of their peers who welcomed additions to their ranks. Gay student groups also could take advantage of the relatively weakened condition of university administrators who were reeling from years of demonstrations, student strikes, and building occupations by black and white student radicals. By 1974, only five years after the birth of gay liberation, almost 175 gay student groups were in existence. Today, in 1985, despite the decline in student activism, the number of such organizations is estimated at 300.[3]

The birth pangs of these groups have not always been easy. In 1970, students at New York University in Greenwich Village had to occupy a university building for a week in order to get university approval for a gay dance. Over the years, gay student organizations have had to fight court battles to overturn the decisions of recalcitrant administrators who had refused them recognition. In New Hampshire, Oklahoma, and Florida, the right of gay students to associate has become a statewide political issue. Moreover, on many campuses, the appearance of a gay student group has provoked harassment and attempts at intimidation from some heterosexual students.

The rationale behind administrators' opposition to gay student groups has been fairly consistent—these groups will encourage activity that violates the criminal law. Almost without exception, however, the courts have sustained the right of gay students to associate. In California, Georgia, New Hampshire, Virginia, Missouri, and South Carolina, to name just a few states that have seen litigation over this issue, judges have reversed the actions of university administrators. These cases have been won because the issue involved a clear violation of First Amendment rights of freedom of speech and assembly—not because courts evinced any particular sympathy for homosexual behavior.[3]

The spread of gay student groups and their victories in court are important indicators of progress. These organizations provide critical peer support for young women and men at a difficult stage in their coming out. They also provide an opportunity to break down stereotypes among the majority student population. In many ways, they serve as a training ground for lesbian and gay youth who will later become proud advocates of gay equality in society at large. Of course, this is precisely why administrators and politicians find these groups objectionable. And it is also why the rights of gay students are so important to defend.

Although the status of gay student groups provides the best evidence of positive change over the last fifteen years, the current situation also illustrates the relative impoverishment of the historical tradition. If we were on the verge of achieving meaningful equality for lesbians and gay men within academia, the question of recognition would have been settled long ago, and there would be gay student groups not simply on a large minority of the nation's campuses, but in every college and university in America. Instead of having to fight for their right to meet in a student lounge, gay students would be working through another, lengthier agenda: the provision of counseling services whose personnel are respectful of a student's sexual choices and encourage self-acceptance; scientific, rather than moralistic, information on sexually transmitted diseases, including AIDS; dormitory counselors who know how to deal with the homophobia of heterosexual students, and university administrators who are prepared to take strong disciplinary action in cases of harassment; curriculum development in the humanities, the social sciences, and the natural sciences so that a college education informs lesbians and gay men about the complexity, variety, and significance of human sexual expression; the guarantee that the activism of gay undergraduates will not later be used against them by university administrators in ways that compromise or restrict their future options. Progress in all of these areas remains rare and exceptional.

FACULTY

When we turn our attention to faculty, we face a situation that is more complex and shows less evidence of progress. Gay liberation could spread easily among students in the early 1970s because of the widespread anti-establishment politics that existed among the young. Moreover, each new entering class of first-year students benefits from the social changes that gay liberation has provoked. Younger men and women are coming of age with models of lesbian and gay pride in the media. They have not internalized to the same extent the fear, the terror, and the habits of discretion that previous generations of lesbians and homosexuals absorbed. Among older tenured faculty, the culture of silence that was once unquestionably necessary for survival remains difficult to break. Among nontenured faculty, the poor state of the job market makes the cost of coming out too high. Staying in the closet is the price that one has to pay for an academic career.

It should come as no surprise, then, that gay male and lesbian faculty have been slower to organize than students and have done so with less success. In 1973, a small group of men and women formed the Gay Academic Union in New York City. In its early years GAU grew rapidly. Its first conference drew 300 people. In 1974 it attracted more than 600, and the following year, 1,200. Chapters have also appeared in many parts of the country. But since the mid-1970s, as the extent of the academic job crisis has become clear, and the political climate has grown more conservative, the numbers have started to decline. And even the numbers that do exist distort one's perception of reality. GAU has always attracted a large number of men and women who are not academics, but who are looking for an alternative to the bars as a way of meeting their educational peers; a disproportionate number of psychologists and therapists who are self-employed; and large numbers of gay men and lesbians who are doing intellectual work outside the academic community.

The reason for the absence of substantial numbers of openly gay faculty members on most university campuses is simple. Discrimination in hiring and promotion is pervasive, even if it is also most often subtle and covert. I know of only one case where a court has supported the suit of a gay faculty member who was fired, and that was because the specific case involved First Amendment issues.[5]

The most revealing evidence about discrimination comes from a 1982 report of the Task Force on Homosexuality of the American Sociological Association.[6] The Task Force sent a questionnaire to department heads around the country and received replies from 640 sociology departments. Only 7 percent reported that awarding degrees to gay or lesbian students would pose a problem. But 63 percent said that hiring a known homosexual would pose serious difficulties, and 84 percent held serious reservations about hiring a gay activist. Forty-eight percent reported barriers in promotion, and 65 percent foresaw problems in promoting activists. Together these 640 department heads reported only thirty-nine lesbian or gay colleagues who are open about their sexuality, and only another forty-five whose sexual preference is known to a small circle.

This, mind you, comes from a profession that in 1969 passed a resolution opposing discrimination against lesbians and gay men in employment.

The situation of faculty also offers the clearest articulation of the contrast between what gay men and lesbians face in the university. Let me speak here impressionistically and from personal knowledge. I know of quite a number of gay male historians who have come out publicly either through their research and writing, or through their work as activists in the profession. I know of far fewer lesbian historians who have done the same, even though my personal acquaintanceship is probably just as great among lesbians as among gay men. The feminist resurgence of the 1960s and 1970s and the growth of women's studies programs have created what at times seems like a parallel structure in the academy. An organization like the National Women's Studies Association provides lesbians with a larger sea in which to swim. It is a place where it is possible for lesbians to find both personal and intellectual support. Yet it is also clear that the precarious position of women within the university structure and of women's studies programs does not allow that personal support to translate into the safety and strength to come out. Women whose scholarship focuses on women's studies are being denied tenure. Under these circumstances, it is risky for lesbian academics to come out in their disciplines.

Still, even in the area of faculty, one has to acknowledge the progress that has been made. In 1970 there was not one openly gay or lesbian college professor in America. To be exposed as a homosexual once meant the certain end of one's career. In the last ten years, gay caucuses have formed in most of the professional associations and are especially active in the Modern Language Association, the American Historical Association, and the American Sociological Association. Some faculty members have come out and have survived.

SCHOLARSHIP

The final area I would like to touch upon is scholarship. If one were to check the card catalog of a major university library and count the books on homosexuality and lesbianism that were published before 1970, the pickings would be very slim. Most of what one would find would be medical literature that reinforced some of the most pernicious stereotypes about gay men and women. Except for some books written in a confessional mode, there were only a few that represented serious intellectual effort: for example, Donald Webster Cory's *The Homosexual in America* and *The Lesbian in America;* Dr. Martin Hoffman's *The Gay World,* which is a study of the male homosexual subculture in San Francisco; and Jeannette Foster's *Sex Variant Women in Literature,* an impressive work of scholarship that Foster had to publish herself.[7]

One of the great achievements of the gay liberation movement has been the explosion of books and articles written by and about lesbians and gay men. There are bookstores in the nation's larger cities that only carry material about the lesbian and gay experience, and mail-order houses that distribute such literature to customers in every corner of the country. There are small independent publishing firms, such as Alyson Publishers and Naiad Press, whose focus is gay or lesbian literature.

Scholars are slowly contributing to this stream of words. In the last few years a number of impressively researched and intellectually significant books have appeared: Dover's history of Greek homosexuality and Boswell's history of the Middle Ages; Faderman's literary study of romantic attachments between women since the Renaissance, and Robert K. Martin's monograph on male homosexual poetry in America; a lesbian studies reader that Margaret Cruikshank has edited, my own book on the homosexual rights movement in the United States, and a sociological study by Susan Krieger of a contemporary lesbian community. The journal *SIGNS* published a special issue on lesbianism.[8] These books and others like them as well as a much larger number of articles are gradually filling in the contours of a neglected aspect of human experience. They also are making it increasingly possible to integrate material about homosexuality into standard courses in a number of disciplines, as well as to construct separate gay and lesbian studies courses.

Although progress in the area of scholarly production is clear, it is worth noting that we are still at the level of tokenism, and not simply because it takes a long time to research and write a book. The same pressures that keep gay and lesbian faculty members in the closet also discourage them, as well as graduate students, from doing work on homosexuality. The study of sociologists that I referred to earlier also had something to say about this: half of the gay sociologists who were interviewed reported obstacles to doing research on the topic and advice that it would hurt their careers. (Sociology, remember, is a discipline with a subfield—deviance theory—that makes the study of homosexuality natural.) In American history, my own book is still the only monograph on homosexuality. There are many excellent topics for dissertations that would make major contributions to our understanding of the American experience, but these dissertations are not being written.

Gay men and lesbians are skilled at turning adversity to their own advantage, and the area of scholarship is no exception. One result of the obstacles to research within the academic community is that many are doing the work anyway and making it a resource for the gay community. Lesbian and gay history projects in Boston, San Francisco, Chicago, Buffalo, and elsewhere are doing an excellent job of researching gay history, and sharing that information within the community through public forums, slide shows, pamphlets, and small-press books. Magazines such as *Conditions, Sinister Wisdom,* and *Gay Sunshine* have published articles that put mainstream scholarly journals to shame. Even gay newspapers carry the work of community-based, grassroots scholars. But creation of successful alternatives should not make us ignore the barriers within the academic community. The university has resources— the libraries, the research money, the legitimacy that wins fellowship support—that lesbian and gay male intellectuals need.

CONCLUSION

Students, faculty, and scholarship. Each of these areas provides evidence of real, positive change over the last fifteen years. Those who remember gay life before 1970 can only think of the changes as nothing short of miraculous. Yet if we look ahead toward the future, toward a vision of equality, it is obvious that the longer part of the road is still to be traveled.

Until now, gay and lesbian students have contributed the most to the quest for equality. It is admirable, and not surprising, that they have done so, but they should not have to carry this responsibility forever.

The expansion of scholarly production is a critical piece of any strategy for equality. Information, education, and ideas are powerful levers for social change, and as we have more information, we will be progressively empowered to act in the world.

But scholarship requires scholars, and that brings me back to faculty, which I consider the weakest link in the chain. Faculty members simply have to come out. Coming out, of course, must be an individual's decision. It needs to be done carefully and thoughtfully, and with a strong support network to sustain the individual. Coming out also involves risk, more in some situations than in others. But much of the danger we perceive does not in fact represent an objective external reality, but our own internalized fears. We need to step through that fear.

In posing this challenge, I especially want to direct it at other white men like myself. We are the ones in this society with the most options. We do not face the added barriers of racial and gender oppression. If we have tenure, of course, we have a degree of security that few Americans enjoy. But even if we do not, we have room to maneuver. Our education has made us socially mobile and opened opportunities. For us, coming out is simply not an overwhelming threat to our survival.

The ideals of our profession demand it from us. The teachers we all remember best, and the ones whom we cherish the most, are those who modeled integrity in the classroom and in their lives, those for whom the search for justice and truth did not represent empty words. We will be failing our students and ourselves if we do not take up this challenge. But if we do seize the challenge, when the time comes to look back and assess our lives, we will be proud of our choice.

NOTES

1. *New York Times,* May 3, 1967.

2. On gay student groups see J. Lee Lehman, ed., *Gays on Campus* (Washington, D.C.:National Student Association, 1975); *Chronicle of Higher Education,* October 20, 1982, pp. 9–10; *Newsweek,* April 5, 1982, pp. 75–77. The current estimate of 300 gay student groups comes from *The Advocate,* 419, April 30, 1985, pp. 12–13. For the context in which these first groups developed, see Dennis Altman, *Homosexual Oppression and Liberation* (New York: Avon Books, 1971); John D'Emilio, *Sexual Politics, Sexual Communities: The Making of a Homosexual Minority in the United States, 1940–1970* (Chicago: University of Chicago Press, 1983); and Donn Teal, *The Gay Militants* (New York: Stein & Day, 1971).

3. The most comprehensive assessment of court cases relating to homosexual rights, including those concerning universities, is Rhonda J. Rivera, "Our Straight-Laced Judges: The Legal Position of Homosexual Persons in the United States," *Hastings Law Journal* 30 (March 1979): 799–956. For more recent assessments of court rulings concerning gay student groups see W. R. Stanley, "The Rights of Gay Student Organizations," *Journal of College and University Law* 10 (Winter 1983/84): 397–418, and A. Gibbs, "Colleges and Gay Student Organizations: An Update," *NASPA Journal* 22 (Summer 1984): 38–41. On April 1, 1985, the Supreme Court sustained a lower court ruling upholding the

right of a gay student group to receive recognition at Texas A & M University. See *New York Times*, April 2, 1985, p. 15.

4. On the founding of the Gay Academic Union, see *The Universities and the Gay Experience: Proceedings of a Conference Sponsored by the Women and Men of the Gay Academic Union, November 23–24, 1973* (New York, 1974).

5. *Aumiller* v. *University of Delaware*, 434 F. Supp. 1273.

6. For a summary of the study see *Footnotes* (a publication of the American Sociological Association), December 1982, p. 1.

7. Donald Webster Cory, *The Homosexual in America* (New York: Greenberg, 1951), and *The Lesbian in America* (New York: Citadel Press, 1964); Martin Hoffman, *The Gay World* (New York: Basic Books, 1968); Jeannette Foster, *Sex Variant Women in Literature* (New York: Vantage Press, 1956).

8. K. J. Dover, *Greek Homosexuality* (New York: Vintage Books, 1980); John Boswell, *Christianity, Social Tolerance and Homosexuality* (Chicago: University of Chicago Press, 1980); Lillian Faderman, *Surpassing the Love of Men* (New York: William Morrow, 1981); Robert K. Martin, *The Homosexual Tradition in American Poetry* (Austin: University of Texas Press, 1979); Margaret Cruikshank, *Lesbian Studies* (Old Westbury, N.Y.: Feminist Press, 1982); John D'Emilio, *Sexual Politics, Sexual Communities;* and Susan Krieger, *The Mirror Dance* (Philadelphia: Temple University Press, 1983). The special issue of *SIGNS* is Vol. 9, Summer 1984.

V
Looking Ahead

Latter-day critics of coeducation have read backward from failures to achieve true equality in the classroom and on the campus to condemn the efforts made by such institutions as hopeless. They excoriate the mixed-sex colleges for their inability to produce a prototype of a truly egalitarian society, one that serves the needs of both men and women, as gendered human beings as well as fellow human beings. But such creative conceptualizations are in short supply in late twentieth-century higher education; dismal demographics and plodding pragmatism ground the flights of imagination even before take-off. Catharine Stimpson's concluding essay, "New Consciousness, Old Institutions, and the Need for Reconcilation" eschews fantasy to argue that coeducational institutions, like the mixed-sex society in which they are located and into which they send their graduates, must acknowledge the reality of a world in which women as well as men make choices about careers, reproductive lives, and the configurations of the families in which they dwell. As she recounts, institutional accommodation to the changing lives of American women may not come easily, but it is only appropriate that coeducational colleges and universities lead the effort.

Today, Americans live in a sexually integrated world, from the boys and girls who toddle together on its playgrounds to the men and women who work together in its boardrooms. Yet between infancy and adulthood, while they undergo their formal education, human beings are introduced into a world of inequality between the sexes. Clearly coeducation cannot create *de novo* a realm of equality any more than any facet of

153

education can alone remedy endemic injustices. Indeed, coeducation, like education, both shapes and is shaped by the society in which it takes place. But men and women can use education, and particularly coeducation, to learn the principles of equality between the sexes and to experience, even within a limited realm, the power of cooperation and mutual respect. The ultimate success of coeducation will not be measured within educational institutions so much as by the health and survival of the larger society.

New Consciousness, Old Institutions, and the Need for Reconciliation

CATHARINE R. STIMPSON

The word "coeducation" originated in the United States around 1874. It names our efforts to educate men and women in the same space, although rarely for the same place. Because coeducation, like education itself, is so immense a social and intellectual responsibility, it has provoked a number of different, and contradictory, philosophies. Let me outline the rough philosophical stance that has shaped my sense of what coeducation ought to be.

In *Beyond Good and Evil,* that scabrous and scandalous polemic, Nietzsche distinguishes between two species of philosophers: the "attempters" or "experimenters" (depending upon one's translator), and the "levelers." The attempters, genuinely free thinkers, are strong enough to comprehend pain; great enough to comprehend the great; deep enough to comprehend the abyss; subtle enough to comprehend the delicate and tremulous; and rare enough for the rare. The attempter is the philosopher for the few.

In contrast, the levelers, deceptively free thinkers, are glib-tongued democrats who believe in equal rights. Tracing the causes of human misery to social structures, they assert that if we but change those structures, we will abolish that misery. The leveler seeks to be the philosopher for the many.

Nietzsche praised the attempter and reviled the leveler. I, however, am a leveler who has learned enough from attempters to suspect utopian dreams that promise to erase all blood and pain from life. I have also had

155

coeducational experiences in public schools and in public and private universities.

My partially coeducated leveler's argument will be that change is a necessary characteristic of postmodern history; that profound changes in our national consciousness are taking place in the United States; that educational institutions of all stripes and sorts are both resisting and encouraging these changes; that intensifying the resistance are the sheer rawness and intricacy of the questions that gender provokes; and that, finally, our new consciousness and our older institutions can cultivate grounds of reconciliation.

The most vital changes in consciousness have to do with our notions of work within school and beyond. Slowly, even excruciatingly, we are degendering them. First, we are recognizing that more and more women of all races and classes are entering the public labor force. By 1990, perhaps only one out of every four women will be a full-time wife and mother. Although occupational segregation still exists, more and more women are entering "male" occupations; between 1971 and 1979, the number of women in male occupations, whether butchers or golf caddies, nearly doubled. In 1962, 19 percent of all college and university teachers were women; by 1971 26 percent and by 1981 35 percent were women. In 1962, 18 percent of all bakers were women; by 1971 30 percent and by 1981 41 percent were women. As this happens, men, though more tentatively, are taking on women's jobs within the home and without.

Next, our theories of human reproduction, women's traditional work, are altering, and this change inevitably affects our sense of the reasons why we are educating women. The twentieth century has seen a vast reduction in infant mortality. In America in 1900, for every 1,000 births, 118 babies died under the age of one. In 1982, for every 1,000 births, 11.5 babies died before their first birthday.[1] This decline in mortality means that parents need grieve less frequently for their dead children. Because the outcome of a pregnancy is now apt to be successful, contemporary women need fewer pregnancies to bear the number of children they want to raise. Because of this, and because of contraception, women, like men, have some separation between sexual expressiveness and reproduction; between pleasure and pregnancy.

Yet in one of those contradictory developments that history so enjoys, even as women have gained greater control over becoming pregnant, the ways of becoming a parent have themselves increased. Technology has given us surrogate mothers; artificial insemination; conception in the

Petri dish; and the vast possibilities of genetic engineering. Woman as womb is being both supplemented and supplanted. It is a sign of our terror at this event that we do everything we can to normalize it. Look, for example, at the media treatment of Louise Brown, the English girl who was the first test-tube baby. The representation of this extraordinary event conventionalized it, anesthetized us to the realities of change. Father Brown was a good worker and provider; Mother Brown a good housewife; Daughter Brown had blonde curls and pretty dresses. The normative, and normal, reigned.

All this reinforces what Paul Robinson, the historian, has called "the modernization of sex."[2] To a degree, we now permit people to choose their sexuality; to unite Eros with a liberalism that praises personal preferences. So doing, we are also more scientific about sex. We study it not as priests nor as prosecuting attorneys but as scientists. For coeducation, the modernization of sex has had the virtues of greater freedom; greater toleration of the activities freedom has permitted; and the placing of sex within a daily context rather than reserving it for "special" times when many repressed desires might gush forth. The dangers for coeducation are the pressures students feel to be sexual in order to seem sophisticated and the possibility that students, under the guise of sexual liberty, are simply dressing up established heterosexual norms.

Still another change in consciousness accompanies the shifts in sexual ideologies and practices: a new awareness of the vast variety of family experiences. Only the willfully blind now say that all families were happy until the New Feminism shattered bowers of bliss. Cain and Abel remind us of the antiquity of sibling rivalry; Oedipus of child abuse. The realistic simply say that the number of contemporary family forms is expanding. More and more people are living alone, in 1980 perhaps 22 percent of all Americans. Even the most solitary cubicle in a college dormitory is paltry preparation for being alone *out there*. More and more, one person heads a family unit. In particular, educators must realize that perhaps a quarter of the first-year students they enroll will come from a family with only one parent at home. If that parent is female, and the chances are she will be, both mother and child may be poor, victims of the feminization of poverty. In California, for example, one year after a no-fault divorce, an ex-husband's standard of living rose 42 percent; an ex-wife's fell 73 percent.[3]

Both reflecting and reinforcing such developments is a new approval in our public ethos, our public beliefs, of individual fulfillment. For we contemporaries are the legatees of Protestantism, American self-reliance, existentialism, and therapeutic interests in the self. Such a heritage makes us less enthralled than our ancestors by a belief that destiny—be it divine, social, or hormonal—shapes character. More and more of us assert that any authority over us must be earned, not assumed. Such assertions necessarily loosen the knot between authority, in and of itself, and masculinity. The same public ethos that praises individual fulfillment finds an ideological correlative in a political preference for democracy and equality over hierarchy. In 1980, for example, immediately after Reagan's victory, a Gallup poll found that 64 percent of its sample favored the Equal Rights Amendment.

Each of these changes of consciousness has helped to create changes in education itself. Among the most striking has been the growth of women's studies. If, in 1969, there were fewer than twenty courses about women in American colleges, by 1985 there were perhaps 25,000 of them. Insisting that women have a new place in academic thought and curricula, women's studies has challenged old errors. It has, for example, shown that women's political participation has involved more than the reigns of Elizabeth I, Catherine the Great, and Lucrezia Borgia.[4] Simultaneously, women's studies has offered both fresh facts about women and new ideas about gender and sexual difference. To give another example, some scholars are arguing that we can unite a theory of profound differences between the sexes, which run beneath specific cultures, with a commitment to political and familial equality. If such scholars are correct, they will be historically unique, for traditionally, in St. Paul or in Darwin at his worst, a sense of irrevocable differences between the sexes has helped to ratify male dominance and female subordination.

It is wrong-headed utterly to condemn American institutions of higher education. Their multiplicity of methods, their democratic range, and their intellectual achievements are massive. Nevertheless, such institutions have in the past excluded, marginalized, and trivialized women. So doing, they have resisted the changes I have outlined. Too often, if they have accepted change, it has been under pressure from individuals, groups, and the government. It was the federal government which, in 1972, passed Title IX of the Education Amendments, which prohibited federal funding of a program or activity that permitted sex discrimination. Indeed, one of my most vivid memories of Columbia University—where I was first a graduate student and then a faculty member at Barnard College—is of a visit that a group of us paid to the president of Columbia. Junior faculty, graduate students, and members of the clerical staff, we possessed spirit but little power. So balanced, we had devised a model affirmative action plan. We walked between two lines of huge, helmeted policemen to deliver the scroll of paper on which we had inscribed our plan to the president. He received it; he dismissed us; we walked back between two lines of huge, helmeted policemen. The paper probably later fed the fireplace in the president's office, but we had made our point.

The forms of institutional resistance have, like snowflakes, had individual structures. However, like snowflakes, they have also shared some common, icy patterns. They have, primarily, tended to express and to perpetuate at least two gender-marked beliefs: that men's work is in the world, whereas women's is at home, and next, that man's active will matters more than women's. As Virginia Woolf remarked ruefully, sardonically, in 1929, in *A Room of One's Own*, no man wants any woman to be inferior. He simply wishes to be superior.[5]

Psychologically, then, young male students have feared professorial authority in female form, and accepted it in male form. Psychologically, too, professors, nearly always male, have exercised their power over students, nearly always female, in the inherently brutal seductions of sexual harassment. Intellectually, despite the gains of women's studies, colleges and universities have often been, at best, diffident about recognizing its validities. The curriculum, our formal organization of reality, may still exclude women and their lives, gender and its influence. Ironically, this resistance has often been more acute in women's colleges than in coeducational ones; coeducational colleges have been more creative about women's studies than the women's colleges that might seem to be their logical source. Structurally, institutions show a resistance to change in their continued willingness to offer the more powerful jobs in teaching and administration to men. They demonstrate a parallel unwillingness to organize child-care, to help parents in the labor force— even though parents belong to student bodies, faculties, administrations, and staffs.

Even when institutions seem to be changing, they may be performing a quasi-magical act and reconstituting old patterns under the guise of new. It is an error to see current coeducation as an oasis of equity and pleasure between high school and the job market. Perhaps there are now more female than male undergraduates, but women outnumber men in only one sort of institution: the two-year college. Unfortunately, the two-year college is the most stigmatized of our institutions of higher education. Women undergraduates are outnumbering men, but only in the least powerful places. Similarly, people cheer when women enter male educational fields. Although their happiness is legitimate, less equity is often there than meets the grossly scanning eye. In 1979, for example, women were 25.8 percent of the students who earned bachelor's degrees in architecture and environmental design. However, they were continuing to earn only 14 percent of the bachelor's degrees in the most "male" activity under that rubric: architecture itself.[6]

Intensifying the tension between a new consciousness and older institutions that confront it is the sheer number of moral questions that such an emerging consciousness provokes. Pricking away at conscience in general, these questions necessarily confront us as we attempt to decide what the ethos of educational communities ought to be. One set of questions, tender and sensitive for students, has to do with the body. Should we be able to do what we want to do with our erotic capacities? Sexually, should we be a genuinely pluralistic society? Moreover, should women be free to choose to do what seems best, not only in terms of Eros, but in terms of their reproductive capacities? Who ought to have power over the womb?

A second set of questions, which involves children, concerns social obligations, with that network of duties that connects any culture or institution, no matter how committed that culture or institution might be to principles of individual freedom. Who ought to raise the young? Who is primarily responsible for the daily well-being of the next generation? In the past women have been, but, as feminists argue, we might be a psychologically healthier and a morally more spacious society if we imposed those responsibilities equally on everyone, be they fulfilled through changing Pampers or paying school taxes. A network of social obligations demands, as well, performing those personal services that sustain everyday existence. The dream that robots might take them over, might benignly and efficiently empty bedpans, sweep school classrooms, fill potholes, brew tea, is another wish for paradise, one that technology has framed. In the past, the powerless—women, the poor, the enslaved, the "lower orders"—have been our robots. However, can we now share onerous tasks without passing them to the humble or creating fantasies of electronic maids and butlers?

Still a third set of questions has to do with that place in which the body and social obligations dash together and interweave: the family. How much do we want the family to embody a commitment to equality? Do we want men and women to be equal centers of being, and of doing, within it? Or do we still demonstrate the sad conclusion of John Stuart Mill, who told us that "the generality of the male sex cannot yet tolerate the idea of living with an equal."[7] Moreover, let us assume, as I do, that children are the equal of adults in terms of their being, their human worth, but not in terms of their doing, their capacity for negotiating with the adult world. If this is the case, how do we best help children through childhood without absorbing a sense of *littleness* that is a psychic source of the acceptance of inequality. Some adults continue to feel small, and thus unequal, while others, seeking to erase the vulnerabilities of childhood, demand and dicker for dominance. As they do so, they choose power over altruism, the sword over the kiss. Even if exercised only at home, their choices flow outward to strengthen a public morality, often linked to masculinity, that prizes strength itself and victory in zero-sum political and psychological games.

Significantly, one of the most suggestive contributions of the new scholarship about women is a body of work, by such people as Sara Ruddick and Alice Rossi, that asks why we cannot base a civic morality on experiences linked to femininity, especially those of motherhood.[8] For mothering, at its richest, helps to generate a genuine capacity for interdependency, affiliativeness, and nurturing. Although the source is mothering, men as well as women can demonstrate such virtues in private and in public. To call for such a demonstration need not be oozily sentimental, nor a pathway to the abolition of the vibrant ego. Few of us long for a future generation of blimps and wimps. Rather, such a demonstration entails the expansion of a public ethos to include the sustaining powers of the maternal role.

None of these moral issues will submit to an easy resolution, in part because people of good will can differ about them. Nevertheless, coeducational institutions are an obvious, necessary, and logical laboratory in which to explore them. Such inquiry can lead to the coeducational college or university as an integrative site in which the new consciousness about gender melds with older institutions. It can be a particularly helpful site if we think of undergraduate education not as an isolated phenomenon but as part of an immense country of learning with provinces reaching from pre-kindergarten through research institutes. In coeducation, we may see if the new consciousness about gender will prove more powerful than fear of change. As the humanistic educational philosopher Maxine Greene has written, "Perhaps a new revolution can . . . take shape, an educational revolution generated by the rejection of sexism."[9] If this occurs, coeducation will realize an ethical promise rooted in its etymology. For the Latin prefix "co" means not strife but mutuality, complementarity.

Graceful ways of incorporating the new consciousness into our older institutions now abound. For example, hundreds of mainstreaming projects, a watery metaphor for a stony job, show us how to bring the new scholarship about women into the curriculum as a whole. Experiments in flex time tell us how to balance work and family life. Perhaps one of the most effective ways of helping coeducational schools is to have a center within each one of them, a presence, with a vigorous interest in women's issues and in gender equity, be it in the curriculum, in institutional life, or in society. Rather than breeding separatism, in which women gather together, away from men, rather than encouraging grumpy mumbles about "The Patriarch," such centers enable women to work on their own behalf and provide ideas and activities for an institution as a whole. Their relationship to gender equity is similar to that of an English department to writing: everyone is responsible for it, but one program specializes in it.

In the nineteenth century, and for most of the twentieth, women's colleges were equivalent presences within higher education. I have had my quarrels with the women's colleges. They have been smug, timid, nervous about sexuality, and pious handmaidens of the status quo. To my embarrassment, the alumnae association of my alma mater refused to endorse the Equal Rights Amendment on the grounds that any organizational endorsement would violate an individual alumna's right to her own belief. Yet the women's colleges have had enormous virtues, and they have supported women and their strengths. Today, fewer than 10 percent of all college presidents are women, but 66 percent of the women's college presidents are. However, only a little more than one hundred private women's colleges still operate, and only a handful of public ones. They are too few in number to embody and to struggle alone for our new consciousness about women and gender equity. Women's centers and women's studies programs within coeducation must supplement them.

To believe in gender equity as a psychological, intellectual, and educational good is to commit one's self to change. However, a great contemporary task is to learn to live in a world in which change is a constant, and to respond to that constant confidently, buoyantly, and deeply. We need to help re-route our nervous circuits so that change does not destabilize us. Simultaneously, a belief in gender equity commits one to a different way of thinking about difference. A western pattern has been to organize human differences of both sex and race hierarchically. White has been different from, and superior to, other colors. Men have been different from, and superior to, women. Any call for equity asks us to accept differences and then, in a far more difficult psychic and cultural task, to organize them as if each element had equal weight and value.

Given how enormous these tasks are, we will need both intelligence and compassion if we are to reconcile our new consciousness and our old institutions. In Shakespeare's *A Midsummer-Night's Dream,* Bottom looks at the chaos around him, at the collapse of the boundaries between fantasy and reality: "Reason and love," he sighs, "keep little company together now-a-days" (III, 1, 147–48). Only if we insist that they keep much company can we create that historical novelty: a genuine coeducation.

NOTES

1. *New York Times* (February 12, 1985), A–17. Such averages conceal the shocking racial differences in mortality rates: for white infants, 10.1 deaths per 1,000 live births; for black infants, 20 deaths per 1,000 live births.

2. Paul Robinson, *The Modernization of Sex* (New York: Harper and Row, 1976).

3. Lenore J. Weitzman, "The Economics of Divorce: Social and Economic Consequences of Property, Alimony and Child Support Awards," *UCLA Law Review* 28 (August 1981): 1251.

4. Jane Roland Martin, "Excluding Women from the Educational Realm," *Harvard Educational Review* 52 (May 1982): 133–48, discusses women's exclusion from the philosophy of education itself. My report, Catharine R. Stimpson with Nina Kressner Cobb, *Women's Studies in the United States* (New York: Ford Foundation, 1986), provides a general survey of women's studies.

5. Virginia Woolf, *A Room of One's Own* (New York: Harcourt, Brace, and World, Harbinger Book, 1957), p. 57. [Originally published 1929].

6. Mary Lou Randour, Georgia L. Strasburg, and Jean Lipman-Blumen, "Research Report: Women in Higher Education: Trends in Enrollment and Degrees Earned," *Harvard Educational Review* 52 (May 1982): 191.

7. John Stuart Mill, *The Subjection of Women* (Cambridge, Mass.: M.I.T. Press, 1970, p. 50 [originally published 1869].

8. For a review of literature about mothers, including Ruddick, see Marianne Hirsch, "Mothers and Daughters," *Signs: Journal of Women in Culture and Society* 7 (Autumn 1981): 200–22. A central Rossi essay is "A Biosocial Perspective on Parenting," *Daedalus* (Spring 1977): 1–33. For comment, see *Signs* 4 (Summer 1979): 695–717.

9. Maxine Greene, *Landscapes of Learning* (New York: Teachers College Press, 1978), p. 254.

Notes on Contributors

JOHN D'EMILIO received his Ph.D. from Columbia University in 1982. He teaches American history at the University of North Carolina at Greensboro. He is the author of *Sexual Politics, Sexual Communities: The Making of a Homosexual Minority in the United States, 1940–1970* (1983). He is currently co-authoring with Estelle Freedman of Stanford University a book on the social history of sexuality in the United States.

JANET ZOLLINGER GIELE is a sociologist and associate professor in the Heller Graduate School at Brandeis University. A graduate of Earlham College, with a Ph.D. in sociology from Harvard University, she has taught at Emmanuel, Wellesley, Radcliffe, and Harvard. Her publications include *Women: Roles and Status in Eight Countries* (1977), *Women and the Future: Changing Sex Roles in Modern America* (1978), and *Women in the Middle Years* (1982). She is currently at work on *Woman Suffrage and Woman's Temperance*, an account of the nineteenth-century feminist movement.

LORI D. GINZBERG received her B.A. from Oberlin College and her Ph.D. in history from Yale University. She is the author of "Women in an Evangelical Community: Oberlin, 1835–50," *Ohio History,* 1980. Her 1985 dissertation is entitled "Women and the Work of Benevolence: Morality and Politics in the Northeastern United States, 1820–1880. She teaches at the University of Rhode Island and is the 1986–87 G. Franklin Jameson Fellow of the American Historical Association.

LINDA K. KERBER is May Brodbeck Professor in the Liberal Arts at the University of Iowa where she teaches history. She is the author of *Federalists in Dissent: Imagery and Ideology in Jeffersonian America* (1970, 1980) and *Women of the Republic: Intellect and Ideology in Revolutionary America* (1980, reprinted 1986), and coeditor, with Jane DeHart Mathews, of *Women's America: Refocusing the Past—An Anthology* (1982). Her research interests are in American intellectual history, especially in the experience of women.

MIRRA KOMAROVSKY is professor emerita and special lecturer in sociology at Barnard College, Columbia University. She is the author of several books on gender roles, including *The Unemployed Man and His Family* (1940), *Blue Collar Marriage* (1967), and, most recently, *Women in College: Shaping New Feminine Identities* (1985)—a longitudinal study of a sample of women undergraduates over four years of college. Professor Komarovsky is a past president of the American Sociological Society and a recipient of an honorary degree from Columbia University.

CAROL LASSER teaches history at Oberlin College. She is the author of several articles on nineteenth-century domestic servants, and has coedited, with Marlene Merrill, *Soul Mates: The Oberlin Letters of Lucy Stone and Antoinette Brown Blackwell, 1846–1850* (1983) and *Friends and Sisters: Letters between Lucy Stone and Antoinette Brown Blackwell, 1846–1893* (forthcoming from the University of Illinois Press). She is currently interested in nineteenth-century woman suffrage organizations.

PATRICIA ANN PALMIERI is assistant professor of education at Dartmouth College. Her interests include the history of women's higher education and the history of women in the professions. She is completing a book entitled *In Adamless Eden: A Social Portrait of the Academic Community at Wellesley College, 1875–1920.*

ALICE S. ROSSI is Harriet Martineau Professor of Sociology at the University of Massachusetts at Amherst. A past president of the American Sociological Association and former chair of the Social Science Research Council, she has published widely on women and gender, including "Equality between the Sexes: An Immodest Proposal" *(Daedelus* 1964), *The Feminist Papers: From Adams to DeBeauvoir* (editor, 1973), *Feminists in Politics* (1982), and *Gender and the Life Course* (1985).

BERNICE RESNICK SANDLER directs the Project on the Status and Education of Women of the Association of American Colleges, the oldest national program dealing with equity for women in academe. Under her direction, the project issued the first paper on campus sexual harassment and the first comprehensive paper on how men and women are treated differently on campus. Sandler also played a major role in the passage and development of Title IX, and in the early 1970s she conceived and spearheaded the successful efforts of the Women's Equity Action League (WEAL) to spur enforcement of the existing Executive Orders regarding sex discrimination in universities and colleges.

BARBARA MILLER SOLOMON, senior lecturer on History and Literature and in the Program on the History of American Civilization at Harvard University, (retired) is author of *Ancestors and Immigrants: A Changing New England Tradition* (1956), *Pioneers in Service* (1956), and *In the Company of Educated Women: A History of Women and Higher Education in America* (1985). Her other publications include editing Timothy Dwight's *Travels in New England and New York* with an introduction (1969); "Historical Determinants in Individual Life Experiences of Successful Professional Women," in Ruth Knudsin, ed., *Women and Success* (1974); "Brahmins and the Conscience of the Community," in *Sacco-Vanzetti Developments and Reconsiderations—1979* (1982); and articles in *Notable American Women* (1971–74). She values highly her success in bringing women's history to Harvard "at least part of the way."

CATHARINE R. STIMPSON is professor of English and director of the Institute for Research on Women at Rutgers University, the State University of New Jersey. Currently the editor of a book series for the University of Chicago Press, she was the founding editor of *Signs: Journal of Women in Culture and Society*. She is the author of a novel, *Class Notes* (1979), editor of six books, and author of more than seventy-five monographs, short stories, essays, and reviews. She currently chairs the New York State Council for the Humanities, the *Ms.* Board of Scholars, and the National Council for Research on Women. Her book on Gertrude Stein and cultural change is under contract to the University of Chicago Press.

MARGARET B. WILKERSON is associate professor of Afro-American Studies and former director of the Center for the Study, Education and

Advancement of Women at the University of California at Berkeley. She holds a Ph.D. in dramatic art from Berkeley and is currently writing a book on playwright Lorraine Hansberry. Among her published works are: "Masks of Meritocracy," "Black Theater in California," "Lorraine Hansberry: The Complete Feminist," *Women at Work: Conflicting Images of Home and Marketplace,* and an anthology of plays by black American women.

Index